WATERLOO ROAD: PAUSELIVEA(

by Sue Haasler

Waterloo Road: Pauseliveaction's Reviews
Copyright © 2013 Sue Haasler

The moral right of Sue Haasler to be identified as the author of this work has been asserted in accordance with the Copyright, Designs and Patents Act of 1988.

All rights reserved. No part of this publication may be reproduced without the prior permission of the copyright owner.

These articles first appeared on the blog www.pauseliveaction.com

The characters and incidents mentioned are the property of the BBC TV series Waterloo Road

School for scandal 6/11/2009 (Series 5)

The start of another academic year at Waterloo Road (if "academic" is a word we can apply to a school that has Steph Haydock on the staff), and there have been a lot of changes. It's merged with some posh school, for a start, and just in case we can't tell the oiks and the toffs apart, they're still wearing their old school uniforms. This makes it easier to spot who's winning when whole-school fist fights break out, as they did fairly regularly in the opening two episodes.

There have been some staff changes. Bob the Builder is no longer deputy head, and Sam Strachan from Holby is some kind of über head, employed to annoy the heck out of head teacher Rachel and fall for the charms of Kim Campbell. There's a feisty new lesbian French teacher (who was last seen walking into the sunset with Abs on Casualty) who has already spotted that Steph can only speak French in the present tense. And there's a rubbish English teacher who has some kind of history with Sam Strachan, which will doubtless be revealed later in the series.

Being a school, several of the older pupils have left, so we've got no Chlo, Donte, Brett, Marley or the wonderful Janeece. Bolton Smiley is still with us, and this week escaped a charge of attempted rape (those posh girls causing trouble). Of the new pupils, the stand-out so far is a cute, curly-haired chappie by the name of Josh Stevenson, who at the end of the second episode revealed that Tom Clarkson may well be his father. (The actor who plays him, William Rush, is the son of Debbie Rush who plays Anna Windass on Corrie, trivia fans).

Lessons we learned this week 12/11/2009

Week 2 of the new term at Waterloo Road, and it's getting really educational. We learned many things this week, including:

1) It's never a good idea to drink anything you find in the science store cupboard. Danielle and her lush hair were in big bother this week after she swigged some ethanol. Steph Haydock was in big bother for ignoring the fact that Danielle was staggering all over the corridor, and just popping her into a cupboard to "sleep it off."

2) Don't wear your cardigan backwards. What was Head of Modern Languages Jo Lipsett thinking when she got dressed? And why did no-one say anything?

3) Don't trust Max Tyler. While I quite like his shouty approach to discipline (it takes me back to my own school days, those halcyon times when kids didn't have any rights and staff rooms were permanently fugged up with fag smoke), I'm a bit worried about Pious Kim Campbell. While Pious Kim's womanly charms are indisputable, I tend to the opinion that Max is just using her to isolate Rachel even more.

3) Don't have a fling with a former member of Smack the Pony (beautiful Fiona Allen) or it will come back to bite you 14 years later in the form of the son-you-never-knew-you-had. Yes, this term's thing for Tom Clarkson to struggle with (there's always something) is the appearance in his life of Josh Stevenson, or, as he must henceforth learn to call him, "our Josh."

4) That Lindsay is a nasty piece of work. Ok, there are extenuating circumstances (her mother killed her father last week and is currently on remand), but as Jeremy Kyle would no doubt say, that's no excuse for writing on someone's forehead.

5) Don't get the same tattoo as your mates. It might seem like a laugh at the time, but when you're 35 you'll just look silly. If it goes septic you'll look even sillier even sooner.

Different strokes 20/11/2009

This week Pious Kim Campbell had her work cut out trying to persuade Executive Head and Boyfriend Max Tyler (or "*Mist*er Strachan!" as I'll always think of him in a Connie Beauchamp voice) to be a little less Wackford Squeers in his approach to discipline. She was right, as well – when you're dealing with a boy who's humiliated because he lives in a care home, it doesn't really help to make him wear a high visibility tabard and pick up litter. All it did in this case was make the boy nick Tyler's car and drive it in circles around the playground in a manner that could surely get him a slot as understudy to the Stig in Top Gear.

    We had a little glimpse into Tyler's persona when he half admitted to the boy that he'd been in care himself. By the end of the episode, he was promising to work a little more co-operatively with the rest of the staff, and snogging the face off Pious Kim to cement the deal.

    Elsewhere, Rose told Josh Stevenson what a diamond of a bloke Tom Clarkson is – why, anybody would be thrilled to have him for a daddy, sure they would. Josh is a little bit spiky about doing father/son bonding stuff, but Tom is winning him round. And Josh is absolutely adorable – what a face!

    And the deeply wonderful Steph Haydock went back to school, for a language teachers' refresher course. When she learned that she may be required to speak actual French to an actual French person, she sensibly scarpered and headed for a nice G&T at home (sweet to see a picture of the late lamented Maxine in her house). Not for long, though, as Jo Lipsett (who wasn't wearing her cardigan backwards this week, I'm relieved to say) flushed her out and made her go back.

Max is married! Steph sleeps with Jo! The cookery teacher cracks up! 26/11/2009

It was open day at Waterloo Road. Everyone had to be on their best behaviour to show the school off at its best for parents and dignitaries.

You just knew that wasn't going to work. Last time there was an open day at Waterloo Road everyone got food poisoning. There were food worries this time as well, mainly due to food tech teacher Ruby Fry having a meltdown when she found out her husband was bankrupt, and hurling crudités ("It's French for chopped vegetables" apparently) around the room before subsiding to the floor in a catatonic state while Michaela White was detailed to clean up around her.

Max Tyler ordered that particular corridor to be cordoned off in case it scared the parents. Another thing he wanted cordoning off was Mrs Tyler. Yes, it turns out that Max is married to the lady from the local education authority. He assigned Deputy Chris to keep her away from his latest squeeze Pious Kim Campbell, but Deputy Chris (who has rather lovely hair) told Rachel the awful truth. Kim is still unaware that she's going out with a two-timing rat. Make that a three-timing rat, as he's apparently also had a "thing" with drippy teacher Helen Hopewell – who is now threatening to blackmail him.

As if all that wasn't enough, Steph decided she really didn't want to go on any more French courses. When she needed to get round former head Jack Rimmer (oh, how I miss him), she always found her womanly charms more than up to the task. As the head of the French department, Jo Lipsett, is gay, Steph reasoned that the very same womanly charms would work equally well. Jo immediately sussed what she was up to, and called her bluff in a very funny scene. By the end, the two were being quite good mates and even went out clubbing together. Then we saw Steph wake up the next morning – next to a sleeping Jo. You didn't need to be a terribly skilled lipreader to work out Steph's reaction.

"Oh. My. God."

Don't stand so close to me 3/12/2009

This week it was the turn of deputy head teacher Chris Mead to be in bother. He's a bit attractive, is Chris, and in a school full of girls with rampaging hormones and only Bolton Smiley as peer group eye candy, he was getting more than his fair share of female attention. IT lessons took on a new dimension as girls spent the time creating animations of his pert posterior for the school website. That sort of thing.

It all got a bit out of hand when one of the girls, a promising chemistry student he was giving extra A level help to, turned out to be moonlighting at a lap dancing club. Chris took it upon himself to save her soul, but almost risked his career in the process. It all turned out fine in the end, and Rachel offered to take him out for a drink. Now she's got over the loss of Bob the Builder, will Rachel's next romance be with the lovely Chris? He does have fabulous hair, so I'm not ruling it out.

Rachel had other things on her mind, though – chiefly, what secret was Lindsey keeping? At the end, Lindsey finally told Rachel about what had been happening prior to her mum killing her dad. Of course we all guessed in week one that the dad had been abusing Lindsey, but Rachel didn't. "If only I'd seen the signs!" she wailed to Chris.

There was a little shock for Tom Clarkson this week, when Josh's mother revealed that a turkey baster had been involved in Josh's conception. Tom is still the father, only kind of one step removed. I'm not quite sure what difference this makes to the scheme of things, but Tom didn't seem happy.

"But enough of all that trivia," I hear you cry. "Did Jo Lipsett and Steph Haydock get it on last week, or what?" A question that Steph herself was quite keen to know the answer to, particularly as the rest of the staff kept making jibes about her manliness. Jo kept her guessing for a while, and then told her that nothing had happened. "Anyway," she smiled sweetly, "I don't fancy older women."

Whore on the door 10/12/2009

Waterloo Road has never shied away from the tricky topics (as anyone who remembers Maxine's baby, Maxine's drug taking, Maxine's death and indeed Maxine generally will testify), and last night's episode dealt with mental illness. Cassie was being bullied – or was she? Pious Kim Campbell thought so, and aided and abetted by Slimy Max Tyler she summoned all the girls for a "no-blame confrontation." Later on the girls took it upon themselves to have a full-blame confrontation in the playground, which is more the Waterloo Road way. Meanwhile, Cassie was behaving more and more strangely, but Pious Kim failed to notice, until Cassie was discovered cowering in the boiler room in terror trying to get away from the voices in her head. "We should have been on top of mental illness!" Kim raged to Max and Rachel and anyone who would listen.

It's not as though Kim didn't have problems of her own, though. Full of happiness because she's in love with Slimy Max Tyler, she just had to tell someone. So who's the last person that you'd confide a secret in? Steph Haydock, that's who. Steph wasted no time in bleating the news to the rest of the staffroom, which of course included Drippy Helen Hopewell, who has history with Max herself. Drippy Helen is so drippy that when she wrote "whore" on Kim's door, she immediately changed her mind and tried to rub it off – but she'd used permanent marker. Oh, Drippy Helen. Kim thought one of the kids must have done it, but that was the least of her worries anyway, as Rachel had just told her that Max was still married to the lady from the LEA. He tried to worm out of it but Kim wasn't convinced. Later, Max paid Rachel a visit at her home, and revealed just what a nasty piece of work he really is.

Elsewhere, Tom Clarkson couldn't look his biological son Josh Stevenson in the eye since he found out that Josh's mother had conceived via a turkey baster. Rose told Tom that he ought to explain to Josh what was going on, so he turned up at Josh's home to deliver the line of the night: "You weren't an accident, Josh – your mother stole my sperm!"

Max Tyler, babe magnet 17/12/2009

Max Tyler really is a nasty piece of work, but for some reason the ladies love him. At the start of the episode, he'd just spent the night with Drippy Helen Hopewell, and all episode long Pious Kim Campbell was staring into space and sighing about him. Have they not noticed Deputy Head Chris? Now there *is* an attractive man.

Drippy Helen was being inspected by a man from the LEA to assess whether she was a fit teacher. She passed the inspection with flying colours – but only because she'd bribed Amy Porter to keep the class quiet. When she refused to carry on with the financial arrangement and was faced with the same class later on (thanks to Max Tyler), Drippy Helen couldn't keep control of the class or herself and ended up slumped across her desk in a sobbing heap. She has now been removed from classroom duties, but left a parting gift for Rachel – the pictures of her and Max together.

So now Rachel knows that Max only gave Helen the job because he was sleeping with her, but what she doesn't know is that Pious Kim Campbell has decided she's really, truly in love with Max and wants to give their relationship another try. After all, she's seen the papers proving that Max is divorcing his wife (which I expect he ran off on the school photocopier earlier).

Tom Clarkson meanwhile was bonding with his son Josh. They've put the inconvenient truth of the turkey baster behind them and shared a "dad & lad" moment at Tom's dad's allotment. And we discovered that Michaela can play the flute. Goshes, who knew?

A pathetic, old-fashioned bully 24/12/2009

Ooh, that Max Tyler is a nasty piece of work, and finally everyone (apart from Pious Kim Campbell) is starting to work it out. His chief tactic is the old divide-and-conquer, setting one person up against another. His chief target was Steph Haydock, and he almost managed to get rid of her. This would have been good news for the teaching profession, but bad news for us, as Steph Haydock is a brilliant character. Luckily Rachel Mason managed to sort everything out, as she's worked Max out for exactly what he is: "A pathetic, old-fashioned bully." She almost managed to wipe the smug look off his face (is it just me who thinks he has a face like a fist?), but not quite. His sort don't let loose of their finger-hold on power very easily.

During the course of the day Max found time to tell Sambucca Kelly that her family were "vermin." Tom's lily-livered reaction to this and his failure to stand up to Max on his girlfriend's family's behalf have led to Rose and Tom breaking up. Rose Kelly may be "vermin," but she's way too good for Tom Clarkson, a man who drifts from one relationship to the next like a jellyfish with stubble.

Max had such free rein to wreak havoc because Rachel was out most of the day, accompanying Lindsay to her mother's trial. The shock revelation here was that it was Lindsay herself who'd killed her father, but hands up anyone who hadn't worked that out already. Get yourselves to the cooler immediately.

Max Tyler gets the boot 1/1/2010

Finally Max Tyler was unmasked for being the odious creep he really is, and the agent of his unmasking was none other than an odious creep from a previous series, Rachel's nephew Philip Ryan. This series he's gone from being a pervy little pest to being a bit more sympathetic, never more so than when he was being bullied by the aforementioned Max. Bearing his bruises with dignity, Philip used the medium of comedy to expose Max for the thug he is, during the end-of-term variety show "Waterloo Road has Talent."

But would pious Kim Campbell believe that the man she loved could be capable of pushing pupils around and trying to oust Rachel? Well, Kim Campbell may be pious but she's not entirely dim, and she's built her career on believing her students, so eventually, yes, she did believe him. Max was confronted in the staff room, and the LEA were informed. The lady from the LEA even showed up personally. You remember her – the one who's married to Max Tyler. What a glorious moment that was.

The upshot is that Max will "probably never teach again" (not that we ever saw him actually teaching – he just snarled at people quietly in corners). So a big sigh of relief all round – Max Tyler is completely out of our lives and not a scrap of him remains. Well, not exactly. He has left Pious Kim with a little souvenir, as she discovered in this episode that she's pregnant. Oh 'eck.

Meanwhile, it wouldn't be Waterloo Road if Rachel let a handsome Deputy Head escape her clutches, and she wasn't about to let Chris go when he drunkenly admitted to fancying her (this was after he'd decked Max for being horrible to her, just because she used to be a prostitute. When will people learn to let that go?). "That wouldn't be a good idea," she told Chris, because she's sensible and professional and she no longer mixes business with pleasure and she sensibly managed to keep her hands off him – at least till the taxi door was shut.

The one with the exploding caravan 7/4/2010

Hurrah! Waterloo Road is back again, and it's as barking mad as ever, being the only programme apart from *Brainiac: Science Abuse* where you can enjoy the sight of an exploding caravan.

I suppose "enjoy" is a bit of a callous word, considering there was someone inside it at the time, but then he had been only moments previously trying to gas his daughter plus her head teacher, Rachel Mason. He'd even wielded a cake knife in Rachel's general direction.

"As of next week, we've just got to focus on putting pupils' emotional health right on top of the agenda," Rachel Mason said afterwards, over a soothing glass of red with deputy (and latest extra-curricular activity) Chris, and Pious Kim Campbell. If they'd only had pupils' emotional health on top of the agenda *this* week, Grantly Budgen may not have allowed a father who had a court order against him from removing his daughter from school and whisking her off to a caravan to possibly do her in.

Pious Kim nodded sagely and sipped a glass of water rather than wine, not because she's pious (which she is) but because she's pregnant. The father of the baby is last term's Evil Headmaster Max Tyler, a control freak who could well turn into a cake knife brandishing psycho at the drop of a hat.

Elsewhere, there's a new pupil in the form of Finn Sharkey (Jack McMullen), an archetypal bad boy who – wouldn't you know – turns out to be a misunderstood and lonely rich kid. In other words, he's Brett Aspinall 2010 style.

And Steph Haydock caught the cookery teacher stealing Jo Lipsett's purse. It's not just the pupils' emotional health that needs putting on the agenda at Waterloo Road.

Making a pig's ear of a school trip 15/4/2010

I watched Waterloo Road last night in the company of my sister, who works in a secondary school. Throughout the episode she made small grumbling noises about how this or that would never happen in a real school – for example the trip to the decrepit farm couldn't have happened without a prior risk assessment and so on. But she still enjoyed watching it. That's the thing with Waterloo Road. It's sometimes almost frighteningly realistic, more often it's like the school on the planet Zog, but either way it's hideously entertaining.

The trip to the decrepit farm yielded a coachload of drunken teenagers, a stolen pig and a kid with chemical burns to his face. By Waterloo Road standards, a fairly successful trip – at least no-one actually died.

The major story arc-type event was Pious Kim Campbell going for her scan, accompanied by Deputy Head Chris. This is Deputy Head Chris who was recently enjoying a passionate encounter with Rachel Mason, but Pious Kim, as we know, is a woman no man can resist for long. Steph Haydock, who likes to keep her finger on the pulse of local gossip, has already spotted that Chris is starting to look a bit besotted whenever Pious Kim is in the room.

Now it's getting silly 22/4/2010

Is it just me, or is Waterloo Road in a bit of a slump at the moment? Last night's episode revolved around Deputy Head Chris Mead deciding one of the girls was Oxbridge material, and needed and deserved special tuition (not in the John Stape from Corrie sense). This brought him into conflict with Pious Kim Campbell, whose motto is "inclusion." Of course, what's really going on is another budding romance. As we've seen with her previous relationships with Andrew Treneman and Max Tyler, what Kim likes most in a man is someone she can argue with. Nothing gets her going quite as much as a good ideological debate.

For some reason (and encouraged by Kim) Michaela White decided she'd try out for the Oxbridge tests. She was fine in the mock interview, but went to pieces in the written exam because she couldn't spell coincidentally. I expected Kim to start railing "We should be on top of spelling!" but she didn't, instead choosing to give Michaela an inspirational lecture of the "just believe and you will achieve" type.

I wish the scriptwriters would make their mind up about Michaela. One week she's a bullying bitch, the next she's playing the flute (not mutually exclusive activities, I realise), the next she's wanting to be businesswoman of the year. Next week she'll probably be back to shoving people round in the playground.

There's a new male cast member in the form of Adam Fleet, the new head chef. He's played by Steven Waddington (who was in one of my all-time favourite films *The Hole* and what's the betting that he won't resist Rachel Mason (whom he knows from her pre-prostitute days) for long?

To me, this series of Waterloo Road has lost its way. There are no strong storylines like the Tom/Lorna/Izzy triangle or the Kelly family. There's far too much Kim Campbell, while nothing much is being done with interesting characters like Josh Stevenson and Jo Lipsett. Next week promises a bit more Josh and a lot more Steph Haydock, which is generally a good thing, so let's hope the series can pick up pace again.

Children can be so cruel 29/4/2010

Another below-par episode of Waterloo Road, with yet again a stand-alone storyline. Young Lauren and The Adorable Josh Stevenson quite fancy each other. However, Lauren has a secret – a large birthmark on her back. This is revealed in front of the whole school during a changing room malfunction at a clothes-swapping event. Everyone laughs and makes nasty comments – even The Adorable Josh, who mainly does it to save face in front of Finn Sharkey, but still.

Normally this would be an excuse for Pious Kim Campbell to swing into action muttering "We should have been on top of embarrassing disfigurements!" However, it was a bit of a low-key episode for Kim, so Lauren was left to deal with her problem by stealing hydrogen peroxide from the science lab in order to bleach the birthmark away. Don't try this at home, folks. Luckily she was tracked down by Tom Clarkson and Chris Mead before any serious harm could be done, and she turned up at Tom and Josh's house later to make friends with Josh again. He's still grounded for his nasty behaviour, though, and Tom Clarkson is wondering whether it's a good idea for Josh to be living with him.

Where was Rachel Mason while all this was going on? Well, she spent most of the episode locked in a food store room with healthy eating guru Adam Fleet (Finn Sharkey's work again). It's hard for any man to resist Rachel, and when locked in a large cupboard with her I imagine it's almost impossible. Adam had apparently hankered after Rachel for years anyway, ever since he was fat. Indeed, she's the reason he got thin. She still managed to resist him though.

And Jo Lipsett is taking the Swotty Kids on a school trip to That London. It's the Swotty Kids, what could go wrong? Two words: Grantly. Budgen.

But that's for another day.

Somewhere only we know 6/5/2010

Has Waterloo Road got the most clueless teachers in the country? I don't mean Grantly Budgen and Steph Haydock – we always knew they were useless, and they never really pretend to be otherwise.

This week Deputy Head Chris Mead was spectacularly useless. Everyone else in Finn Sharkey's year was on work experience, but Finn hadn't managed to get the paperwork signed by his parents. This is, as we know (but the teachers don't) because his parents are away somewhere and Finn is generally Home Alone.

Anyway, Rachel had the bright idea of letting Finn do his work experience in the school, by assigning him as a classroom assistant to work with Chris. Chris and Finn have history, and Finn knows exactly which of Chris's buttons to press. But how someone got to be a deputy head teacher with so little grasp of how to control a classroom, and so little ability to keep his own feelings under control, I have no idea.

Chris has other things on his plate anyway. His dad (Billy Corkhill from *Brookside*) has only gone and left his wife and taken up with that strumpet Steph Haydock. This led Chris to have an amusing fight with his dad in the school corridor, in front of Steph and Finn. "High kicks and girly slaps," Steph sneered. "You're worse than the kids."

Is it any wonder that Finn has zero respect for Chris and spent the rest of the day leading mutinies in the classroom and doing graffiti in the staff room?

Last year's bad boy, Bolton Smiley, has been a reformed character recently, but he almost got into trouble when visiting Sambuca Kelly at the sportswear shop she's doing her work experience in. Sam fancies Bolton (and you can see her point) so she tried to impress him by stuffing an expensive pair of shorts in his bag. When he tried to leave and triggered the security alarm, he and Sam managed to get away. There was a nice little scene on a canal bank, where Sam talked about how hard it was growing up in the chaotic Kelly family (what with her mother being an alcoholic dinner lady, Earl being in prison and Marley never being mentioned any more). They had a sweet little kiss, but as soon as they were back at school Bolton went off with his friend Paul and had to pretend to be tough and macho again.

Ros McCain is supposed to be going out with Philip, the oldest schoolboy in the north (he must be at least 35), but her thoughts have started straying elsewhere. Ros is Waterloo Road's great hope for Oxbridge, and is being mentored by French teacher Jo Lipsett. What with being a French teacher, a lesbian, and having a very weird haircut, we can safely assume that Jo is sophisticated and thrilling. Ros thinks so, anyway, and has taken to gazing adoringly at her mentor. Jo seems to be a more clued-up teacher than most of them, so we'll see how she deals with her star pupil having a crush on her.

She could take advice from Rachel, who is like crush central, as far as men are concerned. Healthy Food guru Adam Fleet is the latest to fall under her dazzling spell. He wants her to have more fun, which he provided this week via the medium of popcorn and a DVD. Steady on there, pleasure-seekers.

Tom and Kim in deadly danger! 27/5/2010

At last Waterloo Road is back on form. This was an excellent episode with a decent story involving regular characters, and pulling in a lot of other storylines as well. And there was no Rachel.

That Finn Sharkey. His name alone, and the fact that he wears the collar of his leather jacket turned up, would give you a clue that he's a Bad Boy. This week, Rochdale's answer to Jim Stark had acquired some legal yet dubious smokeables from the internet, and he and Amy and Josh partook during break time. The effect was to make Amy paranoid, while Josh and Finn went "Whoa!" a lot and looked blissed-out. Then they trooped off for lessons.

When Tom Clarkson noticed that his son was acting a little bit weird, he got all strict with him (Pious Kim Campbell had warned him that he needed to establish proper boundaries), and Josh rebelled by secretly putting the rest of the waccy baccy in Tom's school dinner.

That might have been a bit of a laugh if Pious Kim hadn't needed to rush off to hospital after she started bleeding. Tom volunteered to drive her in his little red car. When Josh realised that his dad was likely to be tripping off his box in charge of a vehicle containing a heavily pregnant lady, he was naturally concerned and Deputy Head Chris was informed.

While Chris was on the phone to Kim, he heard her screaming, brakes squealing, the sound of metal hitting concrete, and all the other worst-case-scenario noises. And worse again, he was right in the middle of trying to persuade a woman from a posh school to let Waterloo Road's oiks use her posh sports facilities.

Anyway... all's well that ends well. Kim and the baby are fine (but Kim doesn't want to be more than "just mates" with Chris). Tom will be fine just as soon as they remove the bandages, and he's forgiven Josh. And the woman from the posh school is throwing open her playing fields to Waterloo Road, thanks to a timely intervention by Steph Haydock, who was seeking to impress Deputy Head Chris (whose dad she is dating).

Ros McCain, meanwhile, is still seeking to impress Jo Lipsett by speed-reading French novels, wearing lipgloss and staring at her from afar (yes, it is a tiny bit stalkerish). She'll be wearing her cardigan backwards next.

That lopsided hair is just too alluring 5/6/2010

Oh, Jo Lipsett. All you did was to give extra-curricular tuition (and this is not a euphemism, it's a literal description) to Ros and take her to see a French film, and now she's all besotted. It must be something to do with your lopsided hairstyle and being a lesbian who can speak fluent French and so on. Compared to Ros's boyfriend Philip, the oldest schoolboy in the north, this must be thrilling indeed.

Chris Mead blamed himself when Ros decided to try and snog Jo, was rebuffed, and then reported her for sexual harassment. It was his idea to have the teachers give extra tuition to the Oxbridge hopefuls, after all. But you have to say that Jo was a tad naive for not sussing what was going on. All ended reasonably well when Ros admitted she'd made it all up.

Pious Kim Campbell would no doubt have emitted a cry of "We should have been on top of lesbian crushes!" but she was busy being grumpy at Chris, who wants to be the latest pilgrim to worship at the shrine of Pious Kim, while she wants to be Just Mates. Or does she? When he had a date with an old Just Mate who may be about to turn into a More Than Just Mate, Kim looked somewhat fed up.

Romance was looking better for Rachel "Man Magnet" Mason, as the latest man she's magnetised, chef Adam, can not only cook but he also wants to spend the rest of his life cooking for her. He's proposed and she's said yes. I do think she should consider whether his lovely ginger hair and beady brown eyes are enough compensation for having him banging on about healthy eating options every five minutes.

Kim has her baby. And Amy is not Banksy 10/6/2010

Haven't the staff of Waterloo Road learned their lesson yet? Never, ever, *ever* take those kids on a school trip. It never ends well.

Last night's trip to an art gallery could have ended up worse, though. Finn stole some art materials for Amy. Shoplifting was his touching way of demonstrating his love for her, though his parents are loaded so presumably he could have bought her a few paints with his pocket money instead. In return, he asked her to deface one of the paintings in the gallery, while he created a diversion by pretending to have a seizure. Oh, Amy. Please just say no to this kind of controlling behaviour – it can only end up with a pramful of babies, a prescription drug habit and an early trip to the Jeremy Kyle studio.

I must say I was very surprised when the gallery let the school off with a mild ticking off and a promise to pay for the cost of getting Amy's scrawl cleaned off the picture. Who'd have thought that art restoration came so cheaply that it would be within the budget of an inner city secondary school? One might almost think it wasn't a real work of art at all, but just a prop quickly thrown together by a bright young thing in the BBC props department. Just saying.

While all this was going on, Pious Kim Campbell was busy going into labour. She had to have an emergency caesarean, which at least meant she was unconscious for a while and unable to worry that "we should have been on top of art vandalism." She woke up to find she had acquired two new men in her life – a baby boy, and Deputy Head Chris Mead, who dumped his current girlfriend to pledge true love to Pious Kim.

Back at the hub of learning that is known as Waterloo Road, everyone was being horrible to Ros because of her crush on Jo Lipsett. Then everyone was being horrible to Philip because he'd slagged the other girls off in a list of Ros's good qualities. Rachel organised a debate about whether boys are better than girls, which came to the shattering conclusion that both genders have a useful role to play in society.

And cookery teacher Ruby moved into a cockroach-infested flat. Best place for her, the annoying, self-pitying whinger. As Kim Campbell wouldn't say.

The cookery teacher finally flips 15/7/2010

After a break of about 30 years to allow for the World Cup, Waterloo Road was back on our screens again last night for the first of two episodes this week (the second is tonight). After that the playground gates will be padlocked once again until the next series.

Last night was mainly about the cookery teacher, Ruby. I never enjoyed cookery lessons at school, but I suspect I might have found them more entertaining if our teacher had been more like Ruby. She's a bit on the edge, is our Rube, self-medicating with drugs purchased on the internet, locking kids in cupboards and developing unhealthy fixations on the head teacher's fiancé.

You can see why Ruby fancies Adam – he's got ginger hair, like her, and an interest in cookery, like her. It's a match made in heaven. Sadly, Adam has eyes only for Rachel Mason, and Ruby's ensuing bout of jealous fury led to her stoving in the top of the wedding cake Adam had just finished icing.

Where was Pious Kim Campbell while all this trauma was going on? She was at home, coping with new baby Dexter, and dumping new boyfriend Chris Mead. Poor Chris Mead – just as well the World Cup intervened, otherwise he'd only have had a week to enjoy the charms of Pious Kim.

School, rather than love, threatened to tear Finn and Amy apart. Following the incident with the spray paint, Amy's parents have requested that she's kept away from Finn during school hours. Despite this, Amy and Finn managed to spend most of the episode gazing into each others' eyes, apart from when Amy was busy helping Ruby wipe wedding cake icing off her wrapover dress.

The school prom – and no-one died 16/7/2010

Finally, Waterloo Road school manages to put on an event without anyone being food-poisoned, the school being set on fire or any of the staff being outed as an ex-prostitute or child beater.

For this reason alone, the end of term prom could be deemed a success, even if it involved nothing more than a plate of cold sausage rolls and a rubbish disco. But it was actually a rather lovely thing, all mirror balls and 1920s-themed glamour (thanks to the efforts of Steph Haydock and the props from last year's school play). Bolton arrived arm-in-arm with Sam Kelly (bless!), and the two were crowned prom king and queen. Steph got back together with Chris Mead's dad. Pious Kim Campbell hasn't completely rejected Chris after all. And Rachel arrived with her brand new husband, chef Adam.

Of course it wouldn't be Waterloo Road without some high drama and anguish. This was provided by Finn and Amy running away to the seaside to commit suicide together, rather than face the prospect of Finn being relocated to Los Angeles by his parents.

It was lucky that Finn (whom I'm reliably informed is "peng") chose the Lancashire coast for this tragic gesture of doomed teen romance. The tide is famously always a v-e-r-y long way out, so it gave Chris Mead time to turn up, spot the star-crossed lovers hand in hand on the beach and leg it across the dunes to catch up. It's a sad comment on the fitness levels of today's teenagers that they were unable to outrun him.

It turns out that all Finn needed was a manly hug from Chris. Having completely career-focused parents who've more or less ignored him since he was seven, Finn's rebelliousness was just the cry for help of a lost boy. Chris took him back to his useless father, had a few sharp words about parenting, and legged it to the Prom. I couldn't help thinking that Finn needed a bit more than that, in terms of counselling and whatnot, but a few sessions with Pious Kim will probably sort him out.

The big end-of-series shock is that Rachel Mason (sorry, Fleet) has decided that Waterloo Road can do without her. She's leaving! And a replacement has already been found – former *Silent Witness* star Amanda Burton. Shame, really – I was hoping Jack Rimmer might come back…

Very moody, even for Rochdale 2/9/2010 (Series 6)

It's the head teacher's job to set the tone for a school. Last term at Waterloo Road Rachel Mason started proceedings by getting herself taken hostage in a caravan that subsequently exploded. This nicely set up a term where we enjoyed art attacks, suicidal runaways, kidnapped pigs and cake vandalism.

New head teacher Karen Fisher is played by Amanda Burton, previously famous for the rather grim *Silent Witness*. It was like she brought a bit of that grimness with her – never before on Waterloo Road have we been treated to such moody music, glowering shots of grey, scudding clouds, bleak moorland... it was more like an adaptation of a David Peace novel than Waterloo Road.

The plot revolved around a small female "genius" who had previously been home-schooled and had a very high opinion of her own intelligence (any teacher other than Grantly Budgen would have been able to pop her facile opinions on English Literature). Having failed to get herself excluded, she legged it out of school and hitched a lift to her dad's house, which was located in the middle of the aforementioned bleak moorland. Her dad had neglected to tell her that he'd sold the house and left. Result – one small genius lost on the moors.

For some reason the entire teaching staff decided to join in the search for her, even though a quick helicopter skim of the area would have found her as she was wearing a bright red coat. It was all an excuse for us to discover Karen's secret anguish – she has a daughter, Bex (Sarah-Louise Platt from Corrie) who has run away from home. The family congregate in her room, under her Joy Division poster, and sigh and wait for a phone call.

Bex isn't Karen's only problem daughter. There's also the lovely Jess, whom we first encountered in the bed of one Christopher Mead. Yup, that'd be Deputy Head Chris Mead. And yup, you can *so* picture his face when he discovered that his latest Miss Alright for the Night was also one of his pupils.

What else is new at Waterloo Road? The marvellous Janeece is back (yay!). She's the new school secretary, and she's also pregnant. Josh Stevenson has had his fabulous hair cut, but as my dad says, there's only two weeks between a good haircut and a bad one, so all he has to do is stay away from the barber's. And there's a new female Spanish teacher, whose style owes more to Nigella Lawson than Dora the Explorer.

Fisher family misfortunes 3/9/2010

After Wednesday's moody series opener, Waterloo Road was back doing what it does best – throwing everything and the kitchen sink up in the air and whipping it all up with a massive wind machine. Metaphorically speaking. They certainly do pack a lot into an hour.

It turns out that Karen Fisher's family is way more dysfunctional than we thought. As well as the missing elder daughter and the teacher-boffing younger daughter, there's also a son who apparently has an eating disorder and a dad who's having an affair. You have to feel sorry for Karen. Actually, you *do* have to feel sorry for Karen, because she's played by Amanda Burton who is a seriously good actress. The scene where she talked to her younger daughter (who blames her for the older daughter going missing) about her feelings was brilliantly written and perfectly acted. "And when I think I've caught sight of her I think, 'I've found you, it's ok.' And then she turns round, and it's not Bex. It's never Bex." Sniff.

Meanwhile, cookery teacher Ruby Fry discovered that she's probably left it too late to have a baby. While drowning their sorrows at the pub and bemoaning the lack of babies for adoption, the Frys were joined by pregnant Janeece, complaining about feeling tired etc etc. Will the Frys want to adopt Janeece's baby? Or, this being Waterloo Road, will it all get a lot more complicated than that?

Anyway, it's all shaping up to be a good term, but several questions are still outstanding, namely:

1 – Will we ever get over the loss of Steph Haydock?
2 – What has happened to Jo Lipsett?
3 – Is Jonah Kirby (Lucien Laviscount) an acceptable substitute for Bolton Smiley?

Another "controversial new initiative" 9/9/2010

Last week we discovered that Waterloo Road had a school nurse. This week, they were determined to use her, and what better way than to conjure up one of Waterloo Road's famous "controversial initiatives"?

Chris Mead, who has stepped into the pastoral care void vacated by Pious Kim Campbell, decided it was a good idea to dispense the morning after pill on school premises, and not before time if the queue at the nurse's door was anything to go by. Of course this is a serious and relevant issue, and the programme tackled it well, unusually featuring a boy (Ronan) who was so concerned about his girlfriend's well-being that he supported her to visit the nurse in the first place, tried to steal the pills for her when she bottled it, and then rang her mum when that didn't work.

The other person in need of a little emergency contraception was the head teacher Karen's daughter, Jess. The Fisher family have gone to pieces since eldest daughter Bex ran away (if they want to see her, she'll be on *Strictly Come Dancing* very soon). Dad Charlie is having an affair with Maggie from *Casualty*. Daughter Jess's moral fibre has come a bit loose. And son Harry spends most of his time binge-eating and throwing up, though no-one has noticed that yet.

Jess feels that, if only Chris Mead could get over this teacher/pupil inappropriate relationship business, they could have a rosy future together. Chris obviously disagrees, being an upright sort of chap. She visited him at his flat, he told her to go home and talk to her mum and popped her in a taxi.

Unfortunately her sort-of friend was lurking in the shrubbery and spotted this, and will be Drawing Conclusions.

Meanwhile Lauren was busy snogging Josh Stevenson, but it seems she could be barking up the wrong tree, as next week it looks like he'll be snogging Finn Sharkey (I know! Sounds random but if you look through tonight's episode the clues are all there).

And Janeece was having second thoughts about keeping her baby. Working at Waterloo Road has given her a terrifying insight into what a handful kids can be.

Josh kissed a boy and he liked it 16/9/2010

After spending last week's episode awkwardly kissing Lauren and looking all ga-ga whenever Finn was nearby, The Adorable Josh Stevenson decided this week to take matters into his own lips and have a go at snogging Finn instead. You can see his point: Finn is kind of adorable himself, he lives in a big posh house and he doesn't giggle all the time like girls do.

Sadly Finn doesn't feel the same about Josh, and got all macho and fighty about it. Not too surprising a reaction, really – he's only a boy, after all. More surprising was the attitude of Josh's father, Tom Clarkson, when Josh 'fessed up that he had actually engaged in a bit of Finn-fondling. Tom Clarkson went all stone-age on him and didn't handle things at all well. By the end of the episode Josh was packing his bags ready to leave, but luckily Tom had a change of heart and apologised.

When Janeece discovered that Ruby Fry was planning to have a baby via surrogacy, she had the brilliant plan that she could give them her baby. She doesn't really like the idea of motherhood, and she does like the idea of letting the baby be raised in "a loving home." However, her visit to the Frys' should have been enough to convince her that if she wants to give her baby up for adoption, she'd be better off going to Becky and Steve on Corrie. Ruby Fry is just plain weird – cold, snappy, obsessive, judgemental, jealous, sarcastic. Not exactly mother-of-the-year material. I'm willing to bet Janeece has a change of heart anyway.

Karen Fisher has thrown her husband out and he's now officially living with Dr Maggie from Casualty. It was missing-daughter-Bex's birthday, and the family commemorated the occasion by sitting round the table gazing at a photo of Bex parked just beyond the flickering birthday cake candles. Jess and Harry think this behaviour is weird and depressing, but it's really so we all recognise Bex when she finally appears in the flesh. The fact that she's Sarah-Lou from Corrie should also help.

Dads. Total embarrassment 23/9/2010

Fathers didn't get an entirely good press in last night's Waterloo Road. Top embarrassing dad of the night was guest artiste Martin Kemp (off of *EastEnders* and Spandau Ballet), who played Ronan's dad. Turns out that the reason Ronan has been the king of the dodgy deal over the last few weeks is not because he's a would-be Alan Sugar. It's because he wants to raise enough money to escape the clutches of his criminal dad, who expects Ronan to join the family "business" of thieving and violence.

Ronan's escape fund was going nicely until it came to the attention of second annoying dad of the night, Marcus (father of Jonah and Ruth), who is now a teacher at WR. Wading in with both feet to try and sort out Ronan's family issues, he very nearly got beaten up for his efforts if Tom Clarkson (more on him later) hadn't intervened. All ended well with Ronan grassing his dad up to the police, who gratefully apprehended him in mid-burglary.

Jess Fisher's dad is an embarrassment as well. Jess discovered this week that he's about to move in with his "fancy piece." "Her name's Maria," said her dad. Oh no it isn't – her name's Maggie from Casualty. Whatever she's called, Jess doesn't want to move in with her.

Tom Clarkson is doing his best to get to grips with son Josh possibly being gay (don't think Josh has quite worked out whether he is or not himself, but he's worked out he doesn't fancy Finn. Only he so *does*). When Josh was getting picked on for (possibly) being gay, Tom decided it would be a brilliant idea to teach him some self-defence moves – in front of the entire class. Not humiliating at all.

It's not just dads who can be really annoying, though. There's always Karen Fisher to represent the annoying mums, though bless her she is trying and has let Jess's friend Vicki move into Bex's room (Jess is keeping a watchful eye on her so she doesn't spill the beans about Jess and Chris Mead).

Ruby Fry isn't even a mum yet, but she's been annoying the hell out of Janeece. Janeece is carrying the baby Ruby is expecting to adopt, and Ruby wants to make sure the foetus gets the best start in life – so she's hovering over Janeece's shoulder being the nutrition police.

They decided to have a full and frank Q&A session, which went hilariously like this:

Ruby: "Father of the baby. Did he look like he had, or may have had, a history of heart disease and/or glaucoma?"

Janeece: "Well, it was dark. And I'd had more than a sniff of sherry."

Ruby: "Fine. Fine. Well, you know, we'll greet any genetic mutations as a pleasant surprise. Your turn."

Janeece: "Was you addicted to tranquilisers?"

Ruby: "Next question."

Who your friends are 30/9/2010

This week's Big Issue on Waterloo Road was drugs. Only it wasn't, really. It was really about friendship, loyalty and doing the right thing.

Amy (who is turning into a right cow) brought some drugs into school. Sam Kelly, who is very anti-drugs because of having an alcoholic mother, decided to get the drugs from her and hand them in. To do this, she borrowed money from Spanish teacher Francesca. It all got very complicated with the real weed being substituted for sage, Sam being accused of all sorts and Karen getting really angry with everyone, particularly the decorative yet useless Francesca. It all worked out in the end when Lauren did the right thing and supported Sam instead of nasty Amy.

Meanwhile, my opinion of Ruby Fry has been completely turned around by this episode. In one of the saddest storylines WR has ever tackled, Grantly Budgen's beloved wife Fleur has Alzheimers. Ruby found her in the cookery cupboard after she wandered barefoot and in her nightclothes to bring Grantly a clean shirt. Ruby was absolutely lovely – by the time Grantly arrived she was gently washing the mud from Fleur's feet and found her some shoes to wear. Grantly is refusing to accept any help from the authorities, because he believes in "in sickness and in health" and thinks it's his duty to cope. Ruby said she'd drop by and bring some cooked meals and do the laundry. Bless her.

We left Grantly and Fleur watching television. She turned to him and said, "Grantly, when can we go home?" His reply was simple but spoke volumes about their situation. "We *are* home," he said. Sad, sad, sad.

Destroying a W of pie 7/10/2010

Front and centre in this episode was Harry Fisher's bulimia, which up till now has been a secret shared only between him and us. When he told his mum that sister Jess was planning to spend the night with school bad boy Finn Sharkey and Jess was grounded, Finn decided to take bullying of Harry to new levels (as a side note, what was Harry doing in the same classes as Finn and Josh? Aren't they older than him?). This culminated in Harry experimentally trying to drown himself during a swimming lesson, but not before he'd snarfed a considerable quantity of quiche which Ruby Fry had lovingly fashioned into the initials "WR" to celebrate the inter-schools debating competition.

Of course, it all had to come out (which I realise could be construed as a tasteless pun, given the subject matter), and Karen went into guilt-and-blame overdrive. She mainly blamed husband Charlie for running off with Maggie from Casualty (who was at Waterloo Road for the inter-schools debating comp, so was very much in the faces of the Fisher family this week). Jess and Harry mainly blamed Karen, for her obsessive hero-worship of missing daughter Bex. They do have a point.

While Karen's anguish occupies large swathes of screen time, you badly need some comic relief, and this was provided by (the very wonderful) Ronan Burley. Now he's got rid of nasty dad Martin Kemp he can get back to ducking and diving, wheeling and dealing like a Rochdale Del Boy. He set up a betting scam on the inter-schools debating comp which could only fail if he himself won. The topic to be debated was school uniforms, and Ronan took the "actions speak louder than words" approach by doing a striptease (or rather "a badly debated point through the medium of interpretative dance," as he styled it) rather than actually debate. And very flexible he is, too. On whose planet did he think that this wouldn't be a crowd pleaser? Presumably he was hoping to be disqualified, but as young Ruth Kirby bottled it, it was either let Ronan win or let the trophy go to a rival school.

The reason Ruth bottled it was because her father puts too much pressure on her to be a genius. She finally got the courage to tell him to stuff his Mensa membership. "Laters!" she told him. "That's not a word!" he yelled – nice to see that some teachers have standards. "It's *my* word," replied Ruth.

And Janeece gave birth to her baby. It was a girl. Prior to the birth she'd decided if it was a girl she'd call her Cheryl, and if it was a boy she'd call it Cole. You can see a theme there. Turned out it was a girl, and Ruby Fry wants to call her Poppy. Poor Janeece – only moments after giving birth she was already apparently out of the charmed circle that was the new Fry family unit.

Where's Pious Kim Campbell when you need her?
14/10/2010

I never thought I'd say this, but I'm missing Pious Kim Campbell, and I think the school is missing her as well. In every episode this series there's been at least one person in need of her finely-honed student support skills (by which I mean her ability to peer intensely at them while beating herself up about not picking up on their problem earlier in the episode).

This week it was the turn of Vicki MacDonald and her lovely eyebrows to suffer in the name of entertainment. Father in a coma following a stroke, mother God knows where, living in a hostel with a hostile room-mate, it was no wonder Vicki's schoolwork was suffering. The ace up Vicki's sleeve was that she knows all about what went on between Deputy Head Chris Mead and headmistress's daughter Jess Fisher; hence she was in a good position to blackmail Mr Mead to adjust her grades when she fluffed an exam.

The scriptwriter piled on the misery for poor Vicki – her classmates found out about her homelessness and were less than sympathetic. I found this a tad implausible – for example Ronan Burley only a few weeks ago was sticking his neck out to do the right thing for his girlfriend, and then stood up to his thug of a father, but was quite happy to be horrible to a girl because she was living in a hostel. Then Vicki was thrown out of the hostel when her nasty room-mate framed her, and then her dad died.

Sitting alone and miserable in a cafe, things looked bleak for Vicki, until the nasty room-mate turned up and gave her some good advice – she should turn to the people who cared about her. Vicki called Jess, who turned up with Chris Mead to get her and take her to a much nicer hostel that Chris knew about.

While all this was going on, Grantly's wife Fleur (who has Alzheimer's) was convinced strangers were trying to steal her "nice things." Grantly is doing his best to help her by himself, labelling everything, leaving meals for her, but it's obviously not enough. She ended up attacking him thinking he was a burglar, and running out into the road and almost getting run over. It's clear she needs more help than Grantly can provide, but as she begged him not to put her in a home, he'll try to carry on.

Ruby Fry is the only person who knows about Grantly's situation, but she was preoccupied this week with looking after baby Poppy. As predicted, though, Janeece is starting to regret giving Poppy up to the Frys. "Just between us," she whispered to the baby, "I'm calling you Cheryl."

I always feel like somebody's watching me 21/10/2010

This week's Chris Mead Controversial New Initiative could also be termed "clunky plot device of the week."

Chris decided, singlehandedly apparently, to have CCTV installed in all areas of the school, including classrooms. No-one else except Chris (and Ruth Kirby) thought this was a very good idea, which begs the question: how did Chris get this past the school governors? Surely on grounds of expense alone it wouldn't be the kind of thing that you would let one teacher do on a whim to "see how it goes"? Never mind the privacy issues.

Ah, the privacy issues. What it was all for, really, was so that certain things which have remained hidden until now were brought out into the open. Jonah Kirby (how gorgeous is Lucien Laviscount, btw? He has a stillness and grace about him which is quite lovely to watch) was less enamoured of the scheme than his sister, and so was dad Marcus, who asked Jonah to compile a presentation about the negative aspects of keeping the school under surveillance. Ronan Burley sneaked a little webcam into the staffroom.

And so it turned out that Jonah finally discovered that girlfriend Jess has had previous carnal knowledge of the aforementioned Deputy Head Chris Mead. Jonah's normally a lover rather than a fighter, but he instantly went off and gave Chris a bit of a battering. Jess begged him not to reveal what it had all been about, and at first he covered for Chris and risked being excluded from school. Eventually Chris had to come clean and tell his boss Karen that he had, indeed, been on an intimate footing with her daughter before he knew she was a pupil at the school.

Once again I felt the programme parted company with reality (I know, I shouldn't be surprised) because Karen decided that Chris could keep his job. A big lapse of judgement on her part. Possibly she just has a soft spot for Scousers, for which I couldn't blame her, but *really* - surely Chris's integrity has been dented so many times in this series that he's beginning to look like a human dartboard?

Meanwhile, the webcam in the staffroom picked up Grantly telling Ruby Fry that Fleur had hit him with a racing book. Fin, Josh, Amy etc all gleefully picked up on this and teased Grantly during a lesson, and were shocked at his reaction – what they didn't know was that Fleur has Alzheimer's and Grantly is only barely coping with looking after her. Ruby realised that Grantly needs help, and called on an old friend – the totally fabulous Steph Haydock (hurrah!). Grantly came home to find Steph and Fleur chatting away happily – only poor Fleur thought Steph was her mum, and didn't know who Grantly was at all.

As if this wasn't heartbreaking enough, Janeece realised that she couldn't give up her baby Cheryl to the Frys after all. Ruby and John had both bonded with the baby (they called her Poppy), so it was a sad situation all round, but Ruby knew that Cheryl should be with her real mother.

Home is where the heart is 21/10/2010

The end of a half term on Waterloo Road, and the school was busy with a fund-raising day. Raffles, dressing up, falafel-eating contests – you know the kind of thing.

Grantly Budgen wasn't getting into the spirit. Not because he's Grantly and therefore a miserable old git who wouldn't give you the steam off his tea, but because he had to face a sad decision. His lovely wife Fleur needed more care than he could provide, and even though he'd promised her he'd never put her in a home, it was the only choice. Luckily for Grantly he had Steph Haydock and Ruby Fry to support him, but he's a proud man and when he discovered that he couldn't afford the home's fees he took the drastic step of trying to burn his house down to get the insurance money. Steph discovered this in time, and he's looking at a singed duvet rather than a spell in Strangeways for arson.

Meanwhile Ruth Kirby had found out that Grantly had been teaching his A level students the wrong syllabus. Grantly's career was on the line, until Steph told Karen about Fleur, and Karen managed to sort out Grantly and his finances in about thirty seconds flat. And when legendary footballer John Barnes turned up to let himself be raffled (there was real fear in his eyes when he was won by Steph Haydock) he promised to double the funds the school had raised on the fund-raising day, and Karen suggested giving it to Grantly. Hurrah!

While this was going on, last week's shady hooded figure was still lurking around, and of course turned out to be Karen's long-lost daughter Bex. Jess discovered her sister lurking in the kitchen at home. Even though they don't much look alike, Jess and Bex are really convincing as sisters, and Tina O'Brien and Linzey Cocker really acted their scenes well, showing all the conflicting emotions of the reunion. Bex said she wasn't staying, and when Karen returned to her office at the end of the day to find Jess looking upset, it seemed as if Bex had done a runner again. "Something's happened," Jess said, and glanced past Karen's shoulder, making Karen turn to find her eldest daughter standing behind her.

So – end of half term report. Overall, much better than series 5, largely thanks to having some strong story arcs throughout the ten episodes. The Fisher family have been a great addition, and I've enjoyed the balance between the storylines of the older cast members and the younger ones. It still manages to bring important and relevant storylines up (such as the one about the morning after pill), with characters you really care about and some fantastic acting so that you don't really mind that you sometimes have to stretch credibility to breaking point.

It's back – the school that puts the fun into dysfunctional
3/2/2011

Waterloo Road is back, in all its barking mad, brilliant, award-winning splendour. And, as usual at the start of (half) term, there are some new faces.

Pious Kim Campbell has been replaced by one Adanna Lawal (Sharlene Whyte). She's suitably qualified for the job of head of pastoral care, as she was previously head of the Dumping Ground in Tracy Beaker, so she knows a thing or two about problem kids. She's not pious like Kim, but she's every bit as stubborn and enjoys contradicting and undermining Karen Fisher and Chris Mead.

This week she was attempting to undermine their latest Controversial New Initiative, which was single-sex classes. In this she was warmly supported by Ruby Fry, who can't maintain discipline at the best of times and only managed to control a class of year 8 boys by drafting in the splendid Janeece to shout at them in their own language.

Ruby's pre-Janeece attempt to interest a class of boys in cookery went disastrously wrong when a fight broke out between new boy Kyle Stack (*Britain's Got Talent* winner George Sampson) and last year's bad boy Finn Sharkey. As it all descended into a food fight, Ruby tried to make the boys stay and clear up the mess, but they headed for the exit anyway as soon as the bell went. "Come here!" Ruby shouted, uselessly tugging at her flowery (and floury) apron. "You're all RUBBISH!"

In a programme which has been outstanding for the quality of its young actors, George Sampson absolutely holds his own. Kyle is the archetypal misunderstood, dragged-up loser who's fallen through the cracks of every system. "School's no use for the job I want," he says. What is the job he wants? "Drug dealing," he reckons, though you sense a lot of it is bluster and there's a sensitive kid underneath. This is confirmed when his beloved Rottweiler Manic is taken away to be destroyed, after Kyle uses him to scare Karen's daughter Bex, who has falsely accused him of sexually assaulting her. His little face when they took the dog away was so sad – if they ever want to remake *Kes*, they need go no further than George Sampson for the Billy Casper role.

On the subject of Bex (Sarah-Lou from *Corrie*), it was her first day back at school following her two year "lost weekend" when no-one knew where she was. And she was getting mysterious texts, phone calls and flower deliveries from someone called "Hodge," which was making her really upset. As usual, Karen failed to notice what was going on with her daughter. Karen calls this "giving her the space she needs." When finally forced to acknowledge that something was wrong apart from back-to-school nerves, Karen sat Bex down for a mother-daughter chat, but Bex refused to say anything about when she was missing. "If I told you, you'd never want to see me again," she said. But it looks like it will all come out anyway before series end, as a mysterious stranger was lurking in the darkness outside the Fisher home.

Other hints of storylines to come came from Jonah rescuing Spanish teacher Ms Montoya from the nasty dog. There's definitely a frisson between these two (Ms Montoya and Jonah, not Ms Montoya and the dog).

And Lovely Josh Stevenson would appear to have a new gay mate whose name is Nate. Finn's not going to be happy.

The art of seduction 10/2/2011

There were various plot strands in last night's Waterloo Road, and two of them (possibly three, if you can conceive of a romance between Grantly Budgen and Ruby Fry) were about romance.

Last week The Lovely Josh met his new gay mate Nate. It seems these two have become close very quickly, to the extent that they're spending most of their time together, and there is most definitely Chemistry between them. As predicted, this hasn't gone down well with Josh's best un-gay mate, Finn, who highlighted a problem I admit I hadn't thought of before. If Josh was going out with a girl, Finn said he'd be ok with it because he'd still be Josh's best mate. But if Josh goes out with a boy, then that boy becomes boyfriend and best mate in one fell swoop, and Finn is sidelined.

Finn is not the Neanderthal he once appeared to be, though, and when Nate turned up at Josh's house while Finn and Josh were having a marvellous time with Josh's Xbox (this is not a euphemism, it's a games console), Finn realised three was a crowd and left them to it. And when the Xboxing was over, Nate asked Josh if he had any more games they could play. Upstairs. He didn't mean Monopoly either.

At school, efforts were being made to get Finn and Kyle Stack to be in each others' proximity without wanting to kick chunks out of each other, via the medium of football. Finn kicked off and kicked himself out of the team, but then changed his mind. Which is just as well, because there was a vital team member missing.

Where was star player Jonah? He was busy having a one-to-one Spanish lesson with Ms Montoya. So far their relationship has not entirely teetered into the classification "unprofessional" but it's a very near thing. Was it entirely necessary for the voluptuous Ms Montoya to place Jonah's hand on her throat so he could feel how Spanish people form certain sounds? And is it any wonder that she later received a text from him saying "I love Spanish!" And was it really a clever idea for her to reply, "Spanish loves you!" Oh, Ms Montoya, it can only lead to trouble.

Trouble was what Janeece was in this week, as she interfered when a friend, who also had a young baby and was returning to school, became convinced that her mother was trying to take her baby away from her. This all culminated in the girl dangling the baby over the top of the school staircase (in a manner that couldn't help but recall that Michael Jackson in Berlin incident). Under the careful questioning of Chris Mead (who was in charge of the school while Karen was away on a course) it turned out that the poor girl was mentally ill, and Janeece's intervention had put her and the baby at risk. Poor Janeece – she always means well, and I love the way she totters round the school in her unfeasibly high heels looking self-important.

Earlier on, Chris thought he heard a baby in the school office. "Janeece – you haven't gone and put your baby in a drawer, have you?" he wanted to know. Janeece was indignant – that would be a foolish and cruel thing to do! The baby was, in fact, in the stationery cupboard. She hadn't wanted to take Cheryl to the creche, because she missed her. You have to love Janeece.

You also have to love Ruby Fry. When Grantly started coming to school all smelly and unkempt, because he was spending all his evenings visiting wife Fleur in her residential home, Ruby took it upon herself to "borrow" his keys and pop round to his house to give it the full *Kim & Aggie*. She stocked his freezer with home-cooked meals, too. And the very loveliest thing – while cleaning she found a little note from Fleur asking Grantly to pick up some eggs on his way home. It was signed "Love you, Fleur." These days, poor Fleur doesn't even know who Grantly is. Ruby ironed the crumpled paper so it looked as fresh as possible, and placed it carefully in front of a photo of Fleur and Grantly, so he found it when he got home. Having that little reminder of Fleur in happier times was precious.

It's those little details that show someone you care, and it's those little details that Waterloo Road does so well.

Hi, Mr Gurney – I'm Josh 17/2/2011

The Lovely Josh and his Gay Mate Nate are in love, and all's right with the world. Except it isn't, because the course of true love is never allowed to run smoothly.

The problem in this case is the parents. Josh has an easy enough time with his dad Tom Clarkson. Tom, despite a few misgivings, is a liberal, easygoing sort of chap who can fairly easily get his head round the idea of his son and his boyfriend spending the night together.

Nate has a tougher time of it with his dad, who is played by Reece Dinsdale (last seen drowning in Windermere on *Corrie*). This being Waterloo Road, a programme that likes to put a little twist on things, Matthew Gurney is not just a raging homophobe (though he is that as well). He's also a man grieving for the loss of his elder son, killed in the army in Afghanistan. When he discovers that Nate is gay, it rips open his grief – in his mind,

Matthew has now lost two sons. Nate, always second favourite son, now has no hope of ever replacing his lost brother.

Nate is torn between loyalty to his father and to himself, and eventually he chooses to be true to himself and to be with Josh (hurrah!). At which point Matthew seeks out Tom, who is attempting a date with Cesca (whose mind is very much elsewhere) – and gives him a nasty battering.

Cesca's response to this, once she's helped Tom stagger home, is to summon a bit of TLC for herself from the beautiful Jonah Kirby. She pronounces his name "Johnner," which is rather sweet. Even though Jonah comes across as being a 39 year old trapped in a 17 year old (or whatever he's supposed to be) body – he has a Zen-like calm to him that makes you fully understand why he'd be the one you'd call if you were feeling kerfuffled – Cesca is of course on very dodgy ground, career-wise. A few of the school staff have already started to notice how much time she's spending giving Johnner private tuition. It'll end in tears.

With all this drama, what you need is a bit of comedy, and you can always rely on Waterloo Road for that. Fabulous Janeece decided to share her wisdom (gleaned by a couple of terms as school secretary), and give classes in the skills of being a PA. She didn't think it was odd that Ronan Burley, Rochdale's answer to Del Boy, signed up and was so keen he asked if he could shadow her as she worked. It was obviously due to her inspirational skills as a mentor. The over-stocked stationery cupboard full of items that no-one had bothered to inventory couldn't have anything to do with it, surely? It wasn't suspicious at all that a boy who is famous for buying and selling anything that isn't screwed down would be taking a large holdall into the cupboard with him.

I love Ronan. He's completely cheeky, but he has his own ethical code as well. He'll sell knock-off DVDs and games, but if you're under 15 he won't sell you anything with a 15 or 18 certificate. And his face just makes me smile.

Ruby Fry and Grantly Budgen are always good for a comedy moment as well. Grantly got tickets for them both to see *An Inspector Calls*, to thank Ruby for her efforts last week. When he caught her reading up on the play in a revision book, he accused her of not being well read. Ruby triumphantly produced a Jilly Cooper from her handbag and challenged Grantly to read it. Adanna caught him quite engrossed in it: "It's interesting from a philanthropic point of view." In return, Ruby has to read *Madame Bovary*, and she's really enjoying it. "I really know how she feels," she says. "Sometimes I feel like a good bit of retail therapy when I'm fed up."

That man Hodge who has been bothering Bex turned up at the school. He also sent Bex an envelope stuffed full of cash. It looks like Bex spent her two year "lost weekend" getting up to some dodgy stuff, but what? My guess is that it's something a bit worse than selling stolen highlighter pens.

Standing up for Dave 24/2/2011

This week Waterloo Road tackled the issue of racism. But it wasn't the rather laboured "Polish people stealing British jobs" theme that got Twitter all-a-twitter last night. It was the relationship between Cesca and Jonah, which "went to the next level." Yes, Jonah started the episode a boy and ended it a man, thanks to the very special private tuition of his lovely Spanish teacher. And, since Jonah is more of a man than most of the men in Waterloo Road, has Lewis Hamilton's hair and a smile that could (and does) light up Rochdale, you can't really blame her. Except you can, because she's a teacher and he's a pupil. It can't end well and it's wrong, I tell you. Wrong. But they do make a beautiful couple.

Meanwhile, who's this "Dave" in the title? It's one Dave Dowling, father to Waterloo Road student Martin Dowling, who is friends with Kyle Stack. When Dave loses out on the job of school caretaker to better-qualified and better-looking Polish person Lukas, he goes into British Bulldog mode and inspires his son and Kyle to "stand up for Dave" by being horrible to Lukas. Frankly it was all a tad heavy-handed and went back to the bad old days of series 5 when a random character was parachuted in for an episode to illuminate an "issue." Ruby Fry took time off from her embryonic romance with Grantly Budgen (they've done *An Inspector Calls*, and now he's taking her to *Oklahoma!* because she likes her theatre to involve show tunes) to add to the racism row by tending to agree that Eastern Europeans shouldn't be taking "our" jobs. But of course our Ruby is not a "real" racist, just a decent sort who's occasionally a tad right wing. Apparently.

Chris Mead was in charge while Karen was away (is Amanda Burton working part-time on this series?) and he got it all sorted out eventually.

While all this was going on, Ronan Burley (who has ingratiated himself into school office life by implementing a brilliant filing concept – alphabetical order. Stunning.) was happily photocopying test papers and selling them to people due to sit the test. Janeece, however, is far smarter than Ronan gives her credit for, and got Grantly Budgen to change the test. There's nothing Ronan likes less than handing out refunds to disgruntled customers.

We still don't know what went on between Bex and Hodge, but she told Jess it wasn't prostitution, so that narrows it down. Hodge was not best pleased when Bex threw all the money he gave her off the roof of a shopping centre, but now he's turned his attention to Jess. Eeek!

And Tom Clarkson is suffering from post-traumatic agoraphobia after being punched by Joe McIntyre from *Corrie*. Poor Josh is at his wit's end, but at least Nate is standing by his man.

Karen Fisher – thick or what? 3/3/2011

The thing about headmistress Karen Fisher is that she doesn't listen. People (her family, mainly) start to tell her things, important things, and she changes the subject, cuts them off, thinks they're talking about something else. She's completely preoccupied with her own stuff, and those around her suffer. So this week the person who probably suffers most of all, son Harry, took it upon himself to cause a bit of mayhem by taking her phone and using it to send messages to her colleagues at the school. By lucky coincidence – or else he's a Machiavellian genius – his emails were all perfectly designed to unsettle their recipients. For example Ms Montoya received an ominous note telling her that a grave matter had come to Karen's attention. Cesca naturally thought this must mean her relationship with Jonah had been rumbled – unthinkable, as they're so discreet. No-one will notice anything as long as it occurs in the bike shed, the art room that is always mysteriously empty, or the cleaning cupboard. Actually, since they only had a caretaker for a day, and they don't seem to have school cleaners, there's probably not a lot of use for that cleaning cupboard.

The messages Ruby Fry and others got had them so upset that Grantly Budgen summoned a union rep, and it was all a good chance for people to tell Karen what they thought of her. Everything got sorted out eventually, and Karen and Harry had a mother/son bonding moment on the stairs and went out for that classic peace-making snack, the pizza.

Meanwhile, as Karen sorted out the problems of her youngest child, middle child Jess was checking into a hotel room with the sleazy Hodge, who is using her to get at sister Bex. It's going to take more than a pizza to sort that lot out.

The plan of segregating boys and girls in lessons is not going well, with the boys falling even further behind. Even a cunning scheme to motivate the boys by getting a local businessman in to run a kind of Dragons Den workshop ended in humiliation for Kyle Stack and a small invasion by the girls, led by Sambuca Kelly, who were angry that they'd been left out. Sadly the best invention they could come up with was a dating website. I know it's worked well for Sarah Beeny, but honestly, girls, there's more to life than romance, particularly when Jonah Kirby is already taken, Bolton Smiley has left, Josh

Stevenson is gay and Kyle Stack is thick and unpleasant. That only leaves a choice of Ronan Burley and Finn Sharkey, and even if they concentrate full-time on romance it's not going to be enough to keep a dating site busy.

Grantly Budgen and Ruby Fry went on a date, in the sense that they arranged to have lunch together and Grantly said "It's a date," as you do. But when Janeece told Ruby that she thought Grantly fancied her, Ruby went all awkward and made a huge point of telling Grantly how much she loved her husband and how she soooooo wasn't looking for a relationship. After her little racist blip last week, Ruby was back on form, and I hope that this little double-act with Grantly keeps going because it's very funny.

This week's sexist 10/3/2011

You thought Kyle Stack was a little toe rag? Ladies and gentlemen, please meet Wayne Bodley (an impressively slimy Qasim Akhtar). Actually, ladies, you may not want to bother, since Wayne is a snivelling sexist pig. And the gentlemen may not want to bother either, for the same reason, and because Wayne is unlikely to be seen again as he seems to be this week's one-episode wonder.

Wayne's presence at Waterloo Road was mainly so what Bex got up to during her "lost weekend" could be spectacularly revealed. Part of Wayne's activities as a snivelling sexist pig involve him having lots of unsuitable material on his phone, and this included a video of Bex. The bits we saw were obviously fairly innocuous, but we were given to believe that it was certainly not the sort of thing you'd want your mum, sister, little brother and the rest of the school seeing. And of course that's exactly what happened.

Every cloud has a silver lining, though, and at least the truth coming out meant that Karen could stand by her daughter (after emoting a bit over Tom Clarkson), and Bex's empowering speech at the Head Pupil hustings got her duly elected. To be fair the competition was poor: Ronan Burley, standing on a manifesto of bribery (with torches that didn't work), stepped out of the contest early to give Jonah Kirby a better chance. He even printed out some leaflets with Jonah looking all buff. But Jonah was too distracted by the double burden of being in love with Ms Montoya, and having to wear a double-breasted cardigan.

Sadly Bex won't be taking up her post, as she's gone off with that nasty Hodge again. This is because Hodge, having slept with Bex's sister Jess last week, now has compromising footage of Jess, which he was prepared to put on the internet if Bex didn't go back to him. But Hodge reckoned without the cunning of Jess, who has finally worked out that the nice man who takes her to hotels and refuses to meet her family (alarm bells ringing, anyone?) is none other than the Hodge who has been threatening her sister. Hodge can expect the combined wrath of a whole load of Fisher folk descending on him... eventually.

It was a better week for Sambuca Kelly. According to PLA Jr, Sambuca is officially the luckiest girl on Waterloo Road, because she's previously snogged Bolton Smiley, and this week got to snog

Finn Sharkey. Finn has swerved from bad boy to being quite the gentleman since Kyle Stack arrived, but it took Sam a little while to notice this. Her mates had spotted that Sam had a love/hate attitude to Finn, and they proved that Tom Clarkson's educational efforts have not been in vain by using Shakespeare to illustrate their point. "Beatrice always gurs on about how much she hates Benedict," said Lauren.

But we've both been so careful! 17/3/2011

Remember what first made Spanish teacher Cesca Montoya notice schoolboy Jonah Kirby in the romantic sense? It was when he rescued her from Kyle Stack's nasty Rottweiler. "Hola," you could see her thinking. "He's all buff and brave and tall and dependable-looking and serene and dazzlingly smiley and that. ¡Ay, caramba!"

What didn't seem to be uppermost in her mind, or just fleetingly anyway, was that she's his teacher, he's her pupil, so basically you just don't go there (although of course Waterloo Road has already gone there several times, what with Davina and Brett and Chris Mead and Jess). Also she didn't factor in that, despite appearances, he's still ever so young.

This week, Cesca started looking a bit peaky in the mornings, and you know what that means. A pregnancy test confirmed that she is, indeed, pregnant with Jonah's baby. Kids having kids, as Jeremy Kyle would tut. Because he's ever so young and crazy in love, Jonah thinks this is all brilliant news, and he can't wait to find himself a job and leave school and start changing nappies, and he *really* can't wait to get very drunk indeed and almost tell all his mates everything.

Luckily (or not), the scene of this drunken behaviour (and I must add that Jonah is *totally* adorable when drunk) was an illicit warehouse party organised by Ronan and Finn, with the express motive of getting Vicky McDonald to snog Ronan. It was successful in that respect, anyway, but went a bit pear-shaped when some dodgy blokes who owned the vodka that had been conveniently left lying around turned up and demanded compensation. Despite them looking like proper hard men, they were no match for Tom Clarkson, who has recovered from his post traumatic agoraphobia and is now perfectly capable of taking on any amount of thugs if they're threatening Our Josh and his boyfriend.

Meanwhile, the Bex/Hodge/Jess storyline finally resolved (thank the lord). When Jess went off in Hodge's car to see Bex, Karen and Chris Mead failed to follow them, but then Hodge got nasty and made Jess wear totally the wrong shade of lipstick for her colouring, so Bex texted the address to her mum. When Chris and Karen turned up, Jess was there but Bex and Hodge had gone. They'd only gone as far as a nearby bridge, where they were fairly easy for Karen to spot from a window, given that Hodge was hauling Bex along by her hair. Luckily a bridge is an excellent spot to form a pincer movement with police at both ends of the bridge, and the evil Hodge was finally captured. Hopefully now Bex will be able to get back to school and getting those all-important qualifications.

Several points to notice:

(a) Ruth Kirby is back, having mysteriously disappeared for several episodes. Let's hope she'll be able to knock some of her famous common sense into her big brother.

(b) Finn Sharkey and Sambuca Kelly split up and got back together again, and

(c) Finn looks very good in beads.

(d) The party was in broad daylight, but what do I know about young people and their ways, or indeed about the problems of night-time filming which may make filming in daytime so much easier.

The Ronan Burley collection 24/3/2011

It was nice to see attention shift away from the Fisher family and on to one of my favourite Waterloo Road characters, the magnificent Ronan Burley. I love Ronan. He's a cheeky chancer, always looking for a money-making opportunity (which quite often fails) and he's a show-off, witness his marvellous striptease in the school uniform debate. But he also has a more serious side – facing up to his bullying criminal of a father, or being responsible about contraception.

This week Ronan showed a flair for makeup and fashion design, in a bid to capture the heart of Vicky McDonald. Ok, so she snogged him last week, but this week an apparently more tempting prize appeared in the form of Ronan's work mentor Dan, played by hunky Will Mellor. A series of misunderstandings, mainly by Vicky and Adanna Lawal, who is turning out to be every bit as pious as Pious Kim Campbell, led to Dan being accused of taking advantage of a schoolgirl. Dan, however, said quite firmly that he "doesn't date children," which makes him quite rare among the adult population of Waterloo Road these days.

While Dan had been busy entertaining Vicky with an innocent pizza and a glass of wine (Wine? During a school day? Dan hadn't wanted to appear "tight" when Vicky said she always liked a glass of wine with her lunch), Ronan was back at school fashioning a piece of haute couture out of a tartan picnic blanket. He wanted Vicky to have something to wear for the fashion show, little realising that she was already wearing a nasty-looking red halter-neck frock that Dan had given her. Ronan's blanket dress was actually quite stylish, and I expect Stella McCartney was sitting at home with her sketchpad on her knee, scribbling away furtively.

Eventually, Vicky decided Ronan was much nicer than Dan – much nicer than anyone, really, particularly with a bit of mazzy on (he was also taking to the catwalk). So to show her love for him, she wore the blanket dress in the fashion show, and everyone loved it, and her team won.

No-one even much minded the big pool of puke in front of the stage. This wasn't down to Cesca Montoya's morning sickness, but down to Harry Fisher, Kyle Stack and Denzil Kelly having a fizzy pop-drinking contest beforehand. What goes in must come out, one way or the other.

Cesca went off to get a termination. It was the sensible thing to do, though "sensible" is not a word we've come to associate with Ms Montoya. Jonah would have gone with her but he had double maths. However, he did leave a message on her mobile phone, and she got the message in the nick of time to realise that, although he's barely out of nappies himself, Jonah could actually make quite a nice father (he'll be able to share his Lego with the little'un) and he makes a very splendid boyfriend. So she cancelled her appointment and headed back to school, where Jonah proposed and she accepted, and they celebrated in their usual discreet way by taking their shirts off in the art room. Where they were – at last – discovered by Ronan Burley. Uh-oh.

Meanwhile, encouraged by Grantly, Ruby Fry decided to have a go at writing a novel. She bashed out a few chapters and presented them to Grantly for his opinion. "Dear God, woman," he told her. "You are depraved! This is filth!" That's a thumbs-up, then.

Cesca and Jonah – the secret is out! 31/3/2011

The thing with Jonah Kirby is, one minute he looks like quite a plausible boyfriend for a 20-something year old teacher (saving her from scary dogs, being a lovely shoulder to cry on after a hard day, being ever so supportive generally and a bit of a hunk). Then the next minute he's kicking a football against the wall, or scrapping with his mates, and he's just a seventeen year-old schoolboy again.

The Jonah/Cesca romance has been interesting in that it's seemed to be a perfectly mutual, completely genuine thing – no coercion, no power games, just a mature young man and an immature older woman getting together against the odds. Proper Romeo and Juliet stuff. Except that we knew it couldn't last, and we knew that Cesca was very much in the wrong in letting her heart rule her head and take her into a taboo relationship with someone who was supposed to be in her care. "No-one was hurt!" she protested to Karen after everything unravelled this week. On the contrary, Karen told her, Jonah has been hurt.

He only started to understand the extent of this in this episode, as he realised that taking his girlfriend on cosy camping trips with his dad and his sister is never likely to be an option. That he may never have the glittering career that everyone predicted for Waterloo Road's star pupil as he has to leave school early and get a McJob to support his imminent offspring. Ronan told him that Cesca looks like a woman who appreciates the finer things in life and wouldn't find life on the dole with Jonah all that attractive. Though PLA Jr pointed out that Cesca's mobile phone is rubbish so maybe she's willing to settle for reduced circumstances after all.

So, considering they've been ever so discreet and only ever had sex in cupboards and the art room in broad daylight, how did the secret romance become public knowledge? Well, it was mainly due to that famous lack of discretion, and Chris Mead having a diploma in body language. He can spot the difference between people discussing Spanish homework and a lovers' tiff even through a fire door. Add this to Jonah's odd behaviour generally, and Cesca's shock resignation (she told Karen her father had had a heart attack and she was going back to Spain, when in fact she was bound for Gretna Green and a quickie wedding with Rochdale's most eligible schoolboy). Chris got the final proof he needed when Cesca fell off a ladder and went to hospital for a check-up, and Chris pulled back the cubicle curtain to find her in a clinch with Jonah, and after that it was a short step to Jonah's father and the police being called and Karen wearing her very best "I'm so disappointed in you" expression (though she always seems to be smiling at the same time, which undermines it somewhat).

Meanwhile, Adanna had come up with this week's New Initiative, which was a gender-bending pantomime called Cinderfella (see what she did there?). This was basically an excuse to showcase George Sampson's running-up-the-wall-and-flipping-over skills, as Kyle Stack auditioned for the lead role and got it, thanks to ninja level dancing skills and winning Britain's Got Talent and everything. Will this be the making of the lad? Possibly. Will Fin "Pantos are for kids and divvies" Sharkey be very, very jealous because Kyle is playing opposite Fin's girlfriend Sam Kelly? You betcha.

Sam should be worrying about her brother Denzil at the moment, though, as he's taken up extreme sports. Not snowboarding and so on, as the opportunities for this in Rochdale are relatively rare, but he definitely has an appetite for adrenaline. Last week it was extreme fizzy pop drinking, and this week he was taking bets on how many volts of electricity he could withstand. It's so nice to see pupils interested in science, isn't it? But luckily for Denzil his friends were a bit concerned about the risk of death, and Tom Clarkson was informed.

Dealing with his former girlfriend's recklessly daft son was a welcome respite for Tom, as he'd been called upon to decide whether Grantly Budgen's rewrite of Ruby's novel was better than her original. Grantly was confident: "You are looking at someone who studied writing while you baked pies," he told his literary adversary. Ruby played to her strengths and baked one of her famous pies by way of a little bribe for Tom. But, pie or no pie (I'll have pie, please), he eventually decided that the winner was... Ruby. And he's an English teacher, so he should know. Though expertise in a subject area has never been a prerequisite of being on the Waterloo Road staff, witness Steph Haydock.

And the bride wore handcuffs 7/4/2011

Another term almost over, and head teacher Karen Fisher sat back in her chair to reflect just how well the term had gone. Both her daughters, Bex and Jess, had been saved from the clutches of a nasty pornographer and son Harry seems to be over his own "issues;" the teacher who'd been caught having an affair with one of her pupils was safely on bail and awaiting trial (and motherhood); Tom Clarkson is healing nicely and is over his agoraphobia; a nasty racist incident was swiftly dealt with; Waterloo Road's first openly gay couple are doing very well; no-one died; and, most importantly, exam results are improving, single sex classes are working, and there's the end-of-term gender-bending pantomime to look forward to!

You could forgive her for cracking open a Bacardi Breezer and toasting a job well done, but, as devoted Waterloo Road watchers will know, the end of term is not the time to relax. It tends to be the time when Something Dreadful Happens.

It usually happens in front of a visiting dignitary as well, so perhaps it was a mistake inviting the chair of governors along to the panto. It was certainly a mistake casting Kyle Stack as Cinderfella. He may have all the dance moves (how Holly Kenny kept a straight face when George Sampson was required to execute a "seductive" body-popping routine in front of her I don't know), but his greatest skill is in winding up Finn Sharkey. Hence the panto didn't go at all to plan, what with Finn and Kyle going toe-to-toe over the lovely Sambuca, Kyle being dumped from the production and Sam going all "you're not a real man" at understudy Finn during the actual performance, when she was meant to be falling for the blinged-up prince.

Jonah (you didn't think I'd forgotten him, did you?) used the panto chaos to escape from the school and rendezvous with Cesca to head for a wedding at Gretna Green. Chris Mead almost managed to stop them, but Cesca persuaded him to wait a crucial few minutes before calling the police: "We love each other and we want to be together – is that so wrong?" "Technically, yes," said Chris, wearing his best sorrowful "Don't do dis" expression.

It's this "technically" that has been the important word. While Karen was at pains to say several times during the episode that Cesca had committed a crime, was morally wrong and had possibly damaged

Jonah in ways he wouldn't understand till he was much older, there's no doubt that the programme's sympathies have been with the star-crossed lovers. Karen David's portrayal of Cesca has been of a naive romantic who let her heart rule her head. Jonah never came across as a victim, but was usually the one driving the relationship forward. This isn't how the courts will see it, of course, but I expect I wasn't alone in thinking how beautiful the bride and groom looked together, and having a tear in my eye when she was led away by the police.

Back in Rochdale, things had taken a dangerous turn. Denzil Kelly, finding that extreme pop drinking and recreational electrocution weren't enough of a "buzz," had taken it upon himself to balance along the wall of a railway bridge, while being filmed by Kyle Stack (being dumped from the pantomime had made him revert to type). Tom Clarkson, Karen, Sam and Finn all rushed to the scene, yelling "Denzil!" or, simply, "DENZ!" repeatedly in an effort to get him to come down, but this only distracted him enough to make him slip. Finn, still smarting from Sam telling him he wasn't much of a man, staged an impressive rescue but then fell off the bridge himself. It looked, to this Casualty viewer, like a skull fracture and spinal injuries might be on the cards. The hospital staff were muttering about "paralysis," and no-one could answer the question of whether Finn will walk again, but he didn't have any form of neck support on in the hospital so I'm optimistic. And Sam has promised to push his wheelchair, a promise which he accepted with such cheerful enthusiasm that I can only conclude he was drugged up to the gills.

And Ruby Fry's book has been published. Look out for *Fairy Cakes* in a fictional branch of Morrison's near you.

Karen's valedictory speech was inspirational. "I see children arrive here completely unaware what they're capable of," she said. And just look what the little monkeys get up to in the space of one term! Luckily Karen feels she has "a lot more to give." Too right. She's had two terms at that school now and she hasn't even had one affair. Rachel Mason and Jack Rimmer would be gobsmacked.

Back to school shocks 5/5/2011 (Series 7)

Waterloo Road started a new, 30 week, run last night at an earlier time slot than usual. The 7.30pm start was presumably to try and hook in some new viewers who haven't been exposed to the delights of our favourite dysfunctional secondary school before.

Anyone who did tune in could have been forgiven for being slightly traumatised come 8.30. Indeed PLA Jr has announced her intention of spending the next few years "wrapped in bubblewrap," as she now feels that being a teenager is just too fraught with danger.

But before we get on to that, what seasoned WR viewers want to know is who's in and who's out. Well, Cesca Montoya, Ruby Fry and Adina Lawal are out on the staff side. New teachers for this term are Eleanor Chaudry (Poppy Jhakra, previously seen on *Corrie*), who is a fierce, no-nonsense Tory who takes no crap from stroppy teenagers or softies like Tom Clarkson (a shame, this, as he's her head of department).

Her polar opposite is Daniel Chalk the maths teacher (Mark Benton), the sort of teacher who practically has "kick me" written on his forehead. He's been taken under the wing of new staff member number three. Robson Green (for it is he, playing Rob Scotcher) may just be an 'umble caretaker (or "site supervisor" to give him his proper title), but he apparently knows more about teaching than you can shake a stick at. I don't think I'm going to get very good odds for my bet that he'll end up being promoted from the cleaning cupboard to the staffroom before very many weeks have passed. Talking of that cleaning cupboard, the Polish caretaker last term had only a small closet as his domain, but Rob Scotcher (will anyone call him "Hop"?) enjoys a bigger room than most of the classrooms to keep his bottles of Jeyes Fluid and his power tools and to flirt with Mrs Fisher (it's time Karen had a bit of love interest, and obviously Chris Mead is out – that would be too spooky, what with Jess and all)

Pupils-wise, Jonah's gone, obviously, as well as Josh's boyfriend Nate (and most of Josh's lovely hair – did he cut it off in grief at the loss of Nate?). Among the newbies are a very amusing pair of twins Shona and Rhona (played by twins Hope and Millie Katana) and Hop Scotcher's son Aidan (Oliver Lee), who is meant to be a hunk but actually looks older than his dad. Obviously Jess Fisher fancies him, but he seems to have his eye on Vicky MacDonald, who is Ronan Burley's girlfriend currently. She'd be mad to dump the wonderful Ronan for him, but we've seen madder things on WR.

Which brings me (I got there in the end) to the plot. We saw a girl in WR uniform abandon a newborn baby in the school. It was later found by Rob, who quietly tried to alert Mrs Fisher, who was giving her traditional start-of-term address to the school. "Discreet" and "Janeece" never belong in the same sentence, though, and pretty soon Janeece was shrieking, "Miss! Someone's left a bay-beh!" And the whole school heard, including Ali (Kirsty Armstrong), the mother of the child.

Kyle Stack thought he was the father, but it became pretty obvious pretty quickly that the real father was Ali's stepfather. And a nasty piece of work he was, too. Karen Fisher sussed what was going on pretty quickly, but she didn't deal with it especially well, choosing to ring the police straight away and leave Ali alone in the hospital, rather than letting the hospital staff know what was going on. Anyway, this gave Ali the chance to leg it with her baby, and she ended up back at Waterloo Road, trying to run away with Kyle Stack. Chris Mead gave chase, but he's not as fast as he was in the days when he could pursue Fin and Amy across Formby beach for hours on end like a gazelle in a cheap suit. He still packs a decent punch though.

Anyway, all's well that ends well, and the nasty stepfather was taken into custody, Ali and her mother were going to deal with things together, and Kyle Stack got over his disappointment at not being a father.

Meanwhile, Sambuca Kelly had been acting strangely all episode, being stroppy and horrible to Miss Chaudry, wearing glasses and producing very bad handwriting. A simple case of a trip to Specsavers being needed, perhaps? Or perhaps not, as the episode ended with her getting a nosebleed in Tom's car and having a seizure in her front garden.

Weepy Wednesday 12/5/2011

It's 7.30pm on a Wednesday evening. You've had your dinner, done the washing up, homework is finished, everyone's winding down nicely and settling down for an evening's telly. And what does Waterloo Road decide to hit you with? A young girl with her life apparently ahead of her, being told that she has a brain tumour and the outlook isn't good. So you're already tugging that box of tissues closer to your chair just in case. Then, to pile on the agony, they throw in the story of a boy who's always felt that he was really a girl, whose predicament makes him bullied, lonely, misunderstood and suicidal.

Then somehow it doesn't turn into the misery-fest it could have done. Somehow it turns into a story of people coming to terms with the hard realities of their lives and deciding they won't give up and give in, but that they'll face it, no matter how hard "it" gets. And people are there to help them.

And somehow, even that doesn't turn out as mawkish as I'm making it sound. It's not one of those golden-sunset, soaring-strings endings from a TV movie on the True Movies channel. It's Rose Kelly getting bladdered on vodka and Tom Clarkson having to sober her up and give her a pep talk about how it's time to finally be the parent to her kids and be a support to Sam as she goes through her treatment. It's Josh Stevenson trying to talk to gender-confused Martin and being knocked back because Martin isn't gay; Chris Mead trying to talk to Martin about the problems of being a normal, hormone-filled lad, and being knocked back because Martin never has felt like a "lad" and never will.

There were pitch-perfect performances all round, particularly from Holly Kenny as Sam. When she told Tom Clarkson that the reason she was back at school rather than in hospital was because she wanted "one more day without everybody knowing," you knew exactly how she was feeling. The scene towards the end where she talked to Martin (Matt Greenwood, also excellent) on the canal bank was beautifully written, and brilliantly performed by both of them. He didn't see any point in carrying on in an existence where he'd never felt he had a proper place, and she faced the prospect of not having much life left and couldn't see why, whatever your problems, you would want to give up if you had a choice to live.

Was there any light relief among all this? Of course there was. We had a stereotype-busting beautician at a careers fair at the school, for one thing. She may have been young, blonde and beautiful, but she was also the head of a small business empire. Even Grantly Budgen was impressed.

Sam's devastating news was made slightly easier to hear (for me at least) because it was delivered by the very lovely Ian Aspinall, formerly Mubbs in Holby. I do miss Mubbs, so it was lovely to see him reincarnated as Dr Kanda. He's in WR again next week, which makes me happy, and with any luck he might decide to wear scrubs.

Something that doesn't make me happy is people messing with Ronan Burley. He's in love with Vicky McDonald (who seems to be getting thinner and browner every week – she's started to resemble an African carved mask). But new lad Aidan has got his eye on Vicky, while pretending to have his eye on Jess. Oh, Vicky, don't go breaking Ronan's heart, or I'll get Very Cross Indeed and set Janeece on you.

Talking of Janeece, she was doing a bit of matchmaking this week between school caretaker Rob and head teacher Karen Fisher. Will his lowly place in the tool cupboard (which is the size of the Starship Enterprise, and he does invoices in there as well because he has brains as well as good looks and an expert way with a claw hammer) stand in the way of love blossoming? The twinkle in Karen's eye would suggest that Rob is definitely in with a chance.

But the episode belonged to Sam's story, and ended with Rose telling Sam that they'd face things together. "This time I'm going to look after you," she said, and they went with Tom to the hospital. And I'm going to need to get another box of tissues.

Heartbreaker 19/5/2011

My usual approach to writing about Waterloo Road is to be all flippant and (ideally) amusing about it. Do they not know how hard they're making it for me at the moment? It's very tricky to be F and A when a beloved character has been smitten by a terminal illness. So let's get the serious stuff dealt with first. This week, Sambuca Kelly discovered that her brain tumour is incurable. She didn't find this out from her mum (who already knew and couldn't think of a way to tell her) or Tom Clarkson (who knew but was too busy ringing round hospitals trying to find someone who just might have a cure that no-one else had thought of). She did a bit of research on the internet then took herself off to the hospital to ask her consultant which of the many pills she was on was going to shrink her tumour. He told her the truth – none of them would. She was dying. Holly Kenny is playing this difficult role with astonishing skill, maturity and honesty. Every tiny emotion is there on her face, and it's quite heartbreaking.

Talking of heartbreaking, what is Vicki McDonald playing at? She was proposed to in front of the whole school (well, a representative selection of regulars and extras, anyway) by the magnificent Ronan Burley. It was all very romantic, with Grantly summing up the joyous mood: "The countdown to teen pregnancy and messy divorce starts now." Then Vicki immediately went off for an assignation with creepy Aiden Scotcher, who is supposed to be way cooler than Ronan because he prefers to spend his weekends grappling with Jess Fisher rather than with a Lord of the Rings box set. Huh. It's going to break poor Ronan's heart when he finds out that his new fiancée has cheated on him, and Jess is not going to be best pleased either, as she spent most of the episode with her tongue lodged somewhere in the region of Aiden's tonsils. What we also know about Scotcher Jr is that he has a bit of a past – his dad warned him that he didn't want to see him "getting another girl pregnant." What are the odds on a baby-mother and offspring turning up at a dramatic moment in a future episode?

Scotcher Senior, meanwhile, has made romantic progress with Karen. She's even helping him with his homework. Yes, it turns out that he not only has a degree, but he's currently studying for a teaching qualification. How terribly handy, given that he's already the best teacher in the school (for a caretaker), if you ignore the health and safety regulations he flouts to get Kyle Stack up a ladder with a squeegee (don't ask). He's already practically on a Dead Poets Society footing with the previously unmanageable Kyle.

Never-Seen-Before-Boy of the week was one Stuart Foley, who was being horrible to Amy Porter (writing "slag" on her locker etc) because her mum was having an affair with his dad and he thought that if he drove Amy from Waterloo Road. her mum would go away too. Deluded indeed if he thinks that he, guest artiste for a week, can get rid of a regular cast member so easily. It all served to show what a peculiarly rubbish teacher Eleanor Chaudery is. She'd been given the Pastoral Care hat for the week, and even by the terrifyingly low standards set by Kim Campbell and Adanna Lawal, she was still rubbish at it.

The mystery girl and the mystery woman 26/5/2011

A bit of a mixed episode, this. A large chunk of it was taken up with one of these stand-alone stories where you know you're never going to see the character again, so it's hard to care. There are exceptions to this, such as the brilliantly-done story of a boy who wanted to become a girl from a few weeks back. Last night's wasn't anywhere in the same league.

Evie was a mystery girl – we knew that Evie wasn't her real name, and we saw a man coaching her about how to respond if people started asking too many questions about her. My guess was witness protection, but it turned out that Evie had drowned her five year old cousin. She'd done the crime, done the time, and was now being reinserted into society without society being made aware of who she was.

Chris Mead found out after about five minutes, but decided not to tell anyone, then when Evie threw a strop and almost strangled Finn (he didn't actually appear to be in any danger), Karen discovered what Chris knew, and got all tetchy about it. I could hear Pious Kim Campbell's voice in my head muttering, "We should have been on top of child murderers!" Karen spent the rest of the shift calming down irate and upset parents.

So far so meh. In between all this, ongoing plots were nicely going on, and, to be fair, the Evie story did shed some additional light on some of them. On what a totally rubbish teacher Eleanor Chaudery is, for one thing. And indeed what a rubbish school Waterloo Road is in the way they handle new pupils. After a quick pep talk about how lovely and friendly the school was, Chris Mead despatched Evie "upstairs" to find her first lesson. Could he not have gone with her? Could they not have appointed a buddy to look after her till she settled in? Instead she was left to face a double bitchy onslaught from Amy and Lauren who thought she was moving in on Finn (she was) in Sam's absence, and she was publicly humiliated by the incompetent Miss Chaudery.

Karen is going to have to sort that Chaudery out. She's even causing trouble for adorable Robson Green! He is quite adorable, though his vowels disturb me. He fluctuates from Geordie to posh and back again in the space of a sentence. But this hasn't put Karen off him, oh no. She even went on a date with him despite staff room gossip (courtesy of Janeece) and Jess claiming that Karen boffing her boyfriend's father would be so, like, *embarrassing*. Little does Jess know that that is the least of her worries re the superficially attractive Aiden. He's still seeing Vicki behind her back (and behind the back of the sainted Ronan – grrr!).

And little does Karen know that a spanner is about to be flung into the works of her lovely new relationship, by the arrival of Robson Green's wife, Frankie Baldwin off of Corrie (Debra Stephenson). She's the mysterious "Naomi" who kept texting him throughout the episode.

The focus of the Sambuca Kelly/cancer storyline shifted this week to the effect it was having on Finn. The poor boy is struggling – one minute he's Jack-the-lad, having fun and messing around with his new girlfriend. The next he's facing dealing with her dying, and the pressure of everyone telling him how much Sam needs him. He had a go at dumping her, but he's made of finer stuff is our Finn, and by the end he was being all huggy and generally brilliant. He told her he'd stand by her whatever happens – and whatever's happening now is that she's decided she doesn't want any more medical treatment.

Every day's just another last time 9/6/2011

I write this through a fog of tears, having just watched last night's episode. Oh my good lord, that was emotional. My usual defence mechanism when it comes to sad things on telly or films is to picture the actors all surrounded by camera people and sound people and so on, but I got so absorbed in Sam's story that I forgot to do that. The result is not a pretty sight.

My cynical side should really have been spending the time ticking off the cliches: final visit to the seaside; attempting to bequeath your boyfriend to your best friend so they can share their grief; going to a funfair and actually winning a cuddly toy; realising that your biological father isn't as important as the man who's always there for you and who loves you. But my cynical side wasn't working, and I'm filling up again, because it was all played out with such sincerity and sensitivity by the main players, and of course particularly Holly Kenny, who's been an absolute star as Sam.

Her death was gentle and quiet and happened while Rose held her and Tom dozed next to them. "It's okay – she's alright," said Rose. "She's alright now." "I fell asleep," said Tom. "Oh, so did she, Tom. She just went."

Oh-oh. I'm going again. Let's move swiftly on to the light relief, which was happily provided by Jodie Prenger (of *I'd Do Anything* fame) playing Linda, a PR lady Karen had drafted in to try and rebrand the school. "Whoever said you can't polish a turd hasn't met me," she pronounced. She proceeded to try and polish the turd that is Waterloo Road by taking lots of carefully edited photographs. The Lovely Josh was deemed a bit too spotty to feature. "Hormones don't sell," Linda told Karen, who replied in her best frosty-knickers voice, "It's a secondary school. Hormones *live* here." Karen wasn't happy with Linda's make-believe portrayal of the school, particularly as she'd decided to feature caretaker Rob Scotcher as the face of the school: "Handsome! Dynamic! Trustworthy!" And back with his wife, presumably dashing Karen's hopes of romance.

Meanwhile, horrible Miss Chaudery had called in the man from the education department, who is not happy with Karen spending money on PR people, and with her dallying with the site manager.

That boy needs neutering 16/6/2011

Sambuca Kelly's time at Waterloo Road will not be forgotten, as she's been given a beautiful memorial of a little tree with a Tupperware box of pens buried beneath it. They were her pens. Sniff. Poor little Denzil has taken to carrying her bright pink hoodie around in his bag (it smells of her), but it was appropriated by a new girl, Scout (Katie McGlynn). We know Scout is trouble because she has greasy hair and she's good at maths. Both of these attributes make her stick out a mile in a school where you can slump glassy-eyed in front of Grantly Budgen all day long, but you must have shiny hair while you do it.

In a scenario which would have Jeremy Kyle frothing at the mouth and spitting out the words "Why didn't you put something on the end of it?" every five minutes, Aiden Scotcher has succeeded in getting not one, but two of his fellow classmates pregnant, apparently in the same week. It's not the first time he's done it, either – we're led to believe that this is why he left his previous school.

He may be firing on all cylinders in the reproductive department, but as a person he's a cringing, oily little worm who runs crying to his mummy when he messes up. When Vicki told him she was pregnant, his first question was "Is it mine?" Her reply was that she and Ronan were "always careful," which I think sums up the contrast between Aiden and Ronan nicely. Not only is Ronan always careful, but even though Vicki has broken his heart he was still willing to take the fall for her when Aiden stole an exam paper so she wouldn't fail it.

Robson Green thinks that Aiden's lack of spine mainly comes from his mother, who runs away whenever there's a problem. She ran away again, horrified by the idea that she could be about to become a double granny. Robson Green thought this meant he could get back together with Karen, but Karen had other things on her mind. She could possibly be about to become a granny herself, as daughter Jess is also in the family way. Karen didn't take this news terribly sympathetically: "Crying won't fix it!" she snapped at her whimpering daughter, who'd taken the sensible step of using waterproof mascara. If only she'd been as well-prepared contraceptively as she is make-up-wise.

I did miss a week of Waterloo Road, so I'm now wondering whether I missed Karen messing up most heinously. The man from the local authority has deemed WR to be a failing school, and Karen to be a failing head – but what, specifically, has she done? Was it just about the murderer who was allowed to semi-strangle Finn Sharkey? Surely in the very long list of Waterloo Road cock-ups, that's not the worst thing that's ever happened? It's all seeming a bit like a clumsy exit storyline for Amanda Burton. We don't want her hounded out for being incompetent. We want her to go in a blaze of glory in an exploding caravan. Well I do, anyway.

Scout's honour 23/6/2011

If doctors make the worst patients, then surely teachers make the worst pupils. Has Chris Mead not learned anything, either from his own life or anyone else's? Look at the mess he got into trying to help out Vicki when she was pole dancing. Look at the mess Cesca Montoya got into when she confiscated drugs and didn't tell anyone. Look at how cross Karen got with him for not sharing his concerns over the mysterious Evie.

But he's got a heart of gold, has our Chris. If we hadn't seen the inside of his flat for ourselves, when Jess was trying to re-seduce him, I would picture it stuffed full of stray kittens and other unwanted pets. He's one of life's born rescuers. This week he tried to rescue Josie "Scout" Allen, she of the unwashed hair and aptitude for maths. It turns out that the unwashed hair etc (but probably not the aptitude for maths) is because she lives with a feckless lump of a mother who is happy for her to supplement the family income by being a drugs courier. And having a paper round.

Let's face it, there's not many teachers would glue your shoes for you. Chris got Scout sorted out with a nice clean Waterloo Road uniform, courtesy of the lost property box, fixed her falling-apart shoes and even provided her with a nice little bag of toiletries so she could get that nasty hair washed. In the changing rooms, and not in the school canteen, where he'd caught her trying to wash her armpits earlier (ugh! Wisest to stick to packed lunches if you go to WR).

He even made sure that, when the police and a sniffer dog arrived following a tip-off by Eleanor Chaudry, the drugs he'd confiscated from Scout ended up in his pocket. Alas, sniffer dogs aren't bedazzled by a cheap suit, a lovely hairstyle and a sincere face, and they can spot a Class B drug when they sniff one. "There must be some mistake," Karen said. "This is my Deputy Head!" The dog ignored her pleas, but the police let Chris go after a talking-to. Karen, however, is not so lenient, and she gave him her best Disappointed In You speech. Then she suspended him. He didn't even have time to say "Don't do dis!" and he was out.

Meanwhile, we learned that the Scotcher family motto is "We Do the Right Thing." In Aiden's case it means publicly humiliating at least one of the girls he's made pregnant. Jess was supposed to be keeping her "condition" on the down-low, but that lasted for about five minutes. After a spot of counselling from Karen (who was taking time out from worrying about being a Failing Head) Jess realised that you shouldn't let a mister come between you and your sister, and she and Vicki made friends again. What fun they'll have at antenatal classes together! Or maybe not, as next week's preview indicated (I'm getting fed up with how much they give away in these previews).

Ronan had a half-hearted attempt at trying to pretend he was interested in Lauren, in order to make Vicki jealous. This backfired when Lauren realised what he was up to and threw water over him.

Will Tom Clarkson throw water over Eleanor Chaudry when he realises that she's been selling Waterloo Road down the river to the smarmy man from the local authority? Yes, the ugly truth is that Ms Chaudry has become the latest in a long, long line of women who find Tom Clarkson irresistible, but is it the first time he's snogged a former Young Conservative?

From now on, it's strictly professional 30/6/2011

Last night's Waterloo Road reminded me of an episode (any episode) of *Brothers & Sisters*, where everyone starts off promising they "won't tell Mom," and five minutes later somebody tells Mom and all hell breaks loose.

Chris Mead didn't promise he wouldn't tell his mom anything, but he did promise Karen that he'd be on his best behaviour, and in particular he'd steer clear of any contact with Scout that wasn't classroom-related. "From now on, it's strictly professional," he told his boss. But that was before Scout's feckless mother (Lisa Riley) decided to have a bit of "me time" by leaving Scout and her three year old brother to fend for themselves while she went on holiday with her latest bloke. Scout couldn't risk not going to school, so she left little Liam parked in front of *In The Night Garden* while she went off to do some gardening herself, courtesy of a community initiative overseen by Kelly Crabtree from Corrie (Tupele Dorgu, whom I would love to see joining Waterloo Road on a permanent basis).

Scout wasn't the only reluctant gardener with thoughts elsewhere. Eleanor Chaudery, who'd been co-opted because a female staff member was needed, was completely out of her comfort zone in wellies. She was a troubled soul, too – it seems that enjoying the pleasures of Tom Clarkson had made her rethink the way she'd been telling tales about Karen to the Slimeball from the local authority.

Meanwhile the Slimeball had told Karen that a member of her staff had been informing on her. Karen looked appalled and stunned, and summoned the faithful Janeece to bring her the passwords of the staff email accounts. It was then a short step to discovering the traitor was – da da DAH! – none other than Eleanor Chaudery.

It all got very tense back at the gardening project, when Chris Mead got wind of little Liam being Home Alone. He and Scout dashed to her home and found the toddler had gone AWOL. There was much rushing up and down and some extremely tense music, until Liam was spotted about to cross a busy road (between parked cars, too – I blame the parents). But didn't.

So did Chris do the right and proper thing and inform the appropriate authorities, including Karen? Like heck he did. He took the well-worn Chris Mead route and decided to handle things himself, by taking Scout and Liam home to stay with him for the night.

When Karen finds out about this, she's going to be super-ropeable, as she was already cross enough because of the Eleanor Chaudery business. Like the schoolteacher she is, she got all the staff together and stared at them hard (more tense music) until one of them 'fessed up to being the supergrass. Of course, Karen already knew it was Eleanor, but there really is no substitute for getting a guilty person to humiliate themselves by admitting everything in front of their peers, as every teacher knows. "I'll deal with you later!" Karen told her. And deal with her she did – by refusing to accept her resignation. What could be a greater punishment than having to keep working at Waterloo Road?

Karen then went off for a showdown with Slimeball, who was also reading from a tried and tested script – this one lifted from a gangster film. "You'll never work in this town again!" he told her. "Your name will be mud in any educational establishment between here and Halifax!" (He didn't actually say that last bit, but that was the gist). I'm still not sure what Karen has done to earn her such a venomous reaction.

Away from the politics and gardening, there was sadness for Vicki, as she lost her baby. "I really wanted that baby," she told Ronan afterwards. "It was going to be my family." One look at Ronan should have convinced her that he was more than ready and willing to be her family. Ben Ryan Davies doesn't get the credit he deserves in Waterloo Road, overshadowed as Ronan sometimes is by the likes of Finn and Josh, who get the meatier storylines. But he can do comedy and seriousness equally well, and he's made Ronan one of the most real and most likeable characters in the programme. It was lovely to see him and Vicki get back together again.

Long live WR! 7/7/2011

Whenever I think of Chris Mead, I shall picture him bounding like a young gazelle across Formby sands in pursuit of Finn and Amy. It was a magnificent feat of athleticism, and one which he reprised in the final episode of this term, as he jogged gamely along the platform at Manchester Piccadilly Station to save Scout and Our Little Liam from evil drug dealer types. Not a hair out of place. Breathtaking. Scout, however, was less impressed. She didn't want to go into "curr." She curred so much about not going into curr that she made Denzil swurr not to tell anyone that she was planning to take Liam, a fistful of drugs money and a packed lunch to That London on a train. But Denzil is a curring type of lad and he's seen the documentaries, so he told Chris what was going on.

Chris's hasty departure from the school premises in pursuit was badly timed for Karen, who was busy trying to impress school inspector Alison (Tracy-Ann Obermann). Throw in Finn, Josh, Amy and Lauren taking a turn around the school car park in Tom Clarkson's car, via the cycling proficiency class helmed by nervous cyclist Daniel Chalk, and you have all the makings of what most school inspectors would term "failure." "Your deputy head just seriously undermined your authority, minutes after four of your pupils were caught joyriding," summed up Inspector Alison. Put that way, it didn't sound good.

The TWOCing of a teacher's car was only a side issue, though (it was Finn's way of expressing his grief over Sam, you know). Inspector Alison was most disturbed by the news about Chris Mead allowing Scout and Liam to use his lovely home as a B&B. She got on the phone to The Authorities, and Slimeball wasted no time in ordering Karen to pack her belongings and get the heck out of Waterloo Road.

So while Chris was busy rescuing Scout from a hideous fate on the Euston-bound platform, Karen was sadly carrying her little box of desk accessories out of the school. But while she'd been packing, the rest of the school had been getting busy, and the entire cast and assorted extras had assembled on the roof and the front steps with badly-drawn placards. They were not going to let Waterloo Road go without a fight. Karen's face as she realised what was going on was an absolute picture – it takes a good actress to maintain that perfect balance between smiling and crying, and the absolute believability of Karen even when all around her is getting pretty ludicrous is why Amanda Burton will be so much missed from the show.

Eleanor Chaudery came good in the end by rounding up her press contacts to give the protest maximum publicity. Kyle Stack came *very* good by throwing an egg at Slimeball. With such a display of solidarity (and throwing accuracy), Inspector Alison had no option but to award the school a positive review, although Karen's future hangs in the balance as she has to wait for a formal meeting to decide if she stays or goes. She ended the episode happily enough, though, in cosy coupledom with newly-qualified teacher Robson Green.

One person who's definitely going is Chris Mead, who admitted to Karen that he'll always be a bit of a renegade and would never learn to play by the rules. He doesn't know what he's going to be doing next, but it could well involve a spot of light jogging.

As well as Eleanor, Aiden also decided to come good. Rattled by the news of Vicki losing her (his) baby, he told Jess he wanted to be a sensible and supportive father for *her* (his) baby. So they went hand in hand into the Rochdale sunset, and I suppose that's the last we'll see of them. When Waterloo Road returns in the autumn, there are going to be a lot of new faces.

Waterloo Road moving from Rochdale to Scotland – but how? 23/8/2011

Waterloo Road is upping sticks from its current Rochdale home, and relocating to Scotland. "Viewers will see a 'dramatic and explosive' storyline played out on screen in early 2012," says the *Manchester Evening News*. "It will result in a number of current teachers and pupils setting up a new school in Scotland, which will also adopt the Waterloo Road name."

Relocating a school to a country with a completely different education system? It's going to take more than an exploding caravan to pull this off. Here are some possible scenarios:

1. England and Wales are engulfed by a tidal wave. Luckily, a plucky young pupil in Waterloo Road's science lab has worked this out well in advance and has persuaded an initially sceptical senior staff team to hire a string of amphibious vehicles to begin the evacuation to the high-and-dry Highlands of Scotland.

2. The Scottish Education Department are troubled by the news that the pass rates in the Highers have increased once again. "How can we ensure that our pupils don't over-achieve?" they worry – and then hit on the perfect solution. Import a rubbish secondary school full of no-hopers like Kyle Stack and appallingly bad teachers like Grantly Budgen, and watch those exam results plummet.

3. The previous seven series were just a dream. The new series starts with Jack Rimmer in the shower (a girl can dream), trying to wake himself up from a nightmare in which Izzy Redpath was stabbed and he eventually resigned from his job, to be succeeded by various women who wore boots with skirts. Realising it was all, indeed, a dream, Jack slips into a rather fetching kilt and heads off through the heather for another day in charge of Scotland's most prestigious and interesting school.

Now I've thought of number three, I'm confident that will be the option they go with. Unless you can think of anything else?

School without doors 15/9/2011

The start of a new school year, and the start of yet another chapter in the eventful life of Waterloo Road. Welcome to the Michael Byrne Era.

He's a new broom sweeping clean, is Mr Byrne. He doesn't like sloppy behaviour – shirt buttons must be fastened all the way to the top and ties pulled up (yes, you, Ronan Burley). Teachers will no longer be allowed to languish behind their desks reading *The Racing Post* (yes, you, Grantly Budgen) – because Mr Byrne has personally removed all the classroom doors, so slackers can be spotted. I say "personally," because caretaker Robson Green is no longer around, so it's not quite clear who does the manual labouring any more.

Every head teacher needs a deputy, but Mr Byrne needs two. One of them is the long-suffering (literally, as he's had at least one bereavement per series since he started) Tom Clarkson. The other is The Radiant Donna off of *Holby City*, only here she's called Sian Diamond. She's still radiant, though, and she and Mr Byrne have A Shared Past. In the present, she's married to PE teacher Jez Diamond, who's only slightly jealous that the headmaster still has a bit of a thing for his wife. And drama teacher Matt Wilding is back, for those *Glee*-style moments that we love so much.

Of the pupils, the magnificent Ronan Burley is still there (hurrah and thrice more hurrah), and he's still engaged to Vicki. Surprisingly, given that it's the end of the summer holidays, Vicki is sporting a more natural-looking complexion and less of the mahogany veneer that was getting a little scary a while back. The Lovely Josh is apparently on a mission to curtail his curls, because his hair is shorter than ever and quite flat. I miss his lovely curls. Finn is sporting stubble and is trying to move on from the loss of Sam by chatting up new girl Trudi.

Trudi's brother is this term's bad boy, Tariq. Arriving at school on The Bus Of The Previously Excluded, Tariq quickly got down to scowling menacingly and taking Ronan Burley's car for an illegal spin in the school grounds. A car being taken for an illegal spin around the school grounds is such a regular occurrence at Waterloo Road that they really ought to have a rally track installed. If only they had a caretaker. They do have prefects, though (who knew?), and Tariq is now one. Mr Byrne feels his leadership skills need to be harnessed for good rather than evil, but we'll wait and see how that works out.

The main storyline revolved around two boys with very big hair, Phoenix and Harley. They were living with their gran, but when she died they decided not to tell anyone, because they didn't want to live with their abusive drunk of a dad (loveable John Thomson, playing against type). This was a very sad story, but I couldn't take it seriously because it kept reminding me of the sketch in the CBBC show *Stupid*, where a granny keeps pretending to be dead to fool her grandson. The boys were friendly with Scout, who is still at Waterloo Road and still currs about people. She curred enough to tell Tom Clarkson, who told Mr Byrne, who went round to advise Phoenix that burying your gran in the garden is both illegal and can ruin your herbaceous border (see, I still can't take it seriously. I kept expecting granny to sit up and say, "Your *face*!").

A totally realistic episode 22/9/2011

We've come to expect Waterloo Road to take quite a few liberties with reality. "That would never happen in a real school" is a frequent refrain. We love it anyway, because the liberties usually fit the story, and the stories are generally gripping and the acting's almost always fantastic, so we can forgive the odd lapse in realism.

But last night's episode was just silly. Let's start with Michael Byrne's A level recruitment drive. Are we really expected to believe that a school would let its pupils make choices about their A levels based on a five minute presentation about how "All computer games start with maths" or "All science is just like CSI"? No matter what your aptitude or your GCSE subjects or results?

Then there was that dreadful "inspirational" speech by Michael Byrne himself, in which his description of how reading a book changed the entire direction of his life (he didn't tell us which book it was. Maybe it was *Catcher in the Rye*, maybe it was *Teaching for Dummies*, who knows?) Any real teenager of my acquaintance would have just sniggered, if they weren't too busy texting.

It didn't take Matt Wilding long to come up with a scheme to bring people together in musical harmony which would result in sulks, strops and theft. In this case it was starting up a school orchestra. He displayed one of each instrument in his classroom and invited people to have a go. This was meant to fire them with a passion for playing the cello/harpsichord/whatever. But the point with most instruments is you can't pick them up and get a decent sound out of them without a lot of practice and probably some lessons from someone who actually knows how to play them. Hence, there weren't many (any) takers for the tuba and everyone wanted a guitar or a drum kit. Well, of course they did. The problem was, there was only one of each. Scout got the sulks because she couldn't have a guitar, so Denzil stole one for her.

We've swallowed all that, but are we really supposed to believe that Ronan Burley has saved up enough money from a Saturday job on a market stall to be able to afford to rent a rather swanky flat with en suite bedroom? We always knew he was a younger and far better looking Sir Lord Baron Alan Sugar, but *really*.

Plot wise, Jez Diamond's kids, Madi Diamond and Zack Diamond, were dumped on him by his ex-wife. He might have walked out on his marriage, but his ex-wife reminded him that Diamonds are forever and not just for Christmas. Zack seems nice enough, but that Madi is a bit of a handful. I particularly liked her trick of harvesting hair from the hairbrush to put in the soup. The highlight of the evening was seeing Janeece cough this up like a cat expelling a fur ball. She's a classy act, that Janeece.

And Michael Byrne tried to get big haired brothers Phoenix and Harley to bond with their dad, loveable comedian John Thomson.

Is it just me? 10/10/2011

I'm having trouble with this series of Waterloo Road. Basically, I'm wondering how much longer I should give the new characters to bed in. Is it just a matter of time before Michael Byrne, the Diamonds and the terrible Sarah Hadland character start seeming like proper Waterloo Road teachers?

I love Jaye Jacobs, I adored and revered her as The Radiant Donna in *Holby City*, but something about her character isn't working in this. I don't think it's the actress's fault. As Donna, she was given a part that was funny, vulnerable and sweet. She could be selfish, stroppy and lazy, but we always cared about her. I just don't care about Sian Diamond, even though I do rather love the dresses she wears. Jez is neither here nor there – not a serious character, not a comic character (so he's had Botox? Big deal). And Michael Byrne is a cardboard cutout of a headmaster, not fit to fill the shoes of Jack Rimmer, Rachel Mason and Karen Fisher.

Did I hate the last episode, then? Well, no, because a lot of it featured the glorious Ronan Burley, my favourite Waterloo Road character. Maybe I'm just against Sian for daring to suggest that Our Ronan could ever hit Vicki. It's almost as absurd as thinking he could captain a rugby team.

But I'm hankering after the mad old days of Ruby Fry having a meltdown in the cookery room, and Grantly and Fleur, and Steph Haydock, and Pious Kim Campbell, and Chris Mead coming up with Controversial New Initiatives. Poor old Daniel Chalk and his winning ways with an electric guitar just aren't providing a sufficient level of that particular kind of warm barminess that WR specialises in.

Or is it just me?

The Jeremy Kyle holding pen 21/10/2011

Finn Sharkey has managed to put his heartbreak over losing Sam to one side. After a short wobble when grief made him steal cars and drive them round the playground, he's back on the dating scene with a spring in his step. Sadly his choice of new girlfriend is Trudi Siddiqui. While it's true she's beautiful and smart, she has one big drawback. Her brother is a nutter. He's also the only prefect in the school, but that's Michael Byrne's idea of giving the lad responsibility. Does this make Tariq Siddiqui the head boy by default?

For a while, a nice little bromance was brewing between Tariq and Finn, but this only held for as long as Tariq remained blissfully ignorant about Finn's designs on his sister. They even went out together to do a spot of revenge beating up of some lads who'd stolen Madi Diamond's phone. En route to the beating up (Tariq knows jiu jitsu, you know. Like Keanu Reeves in *The Matrix*, only Keanu didn't learn it in a Young Offenders Institute) Tariq admitted that Her Majesty's Pleasure hadn't been all that pleasurable. Finn already knew this, as Trudi had told him Tariq spent most of his sentence crying down the phone to his mum.

You just knew it would be about five minutes before that news got out (Ronan Burley, I'm disappointed in you), along with the news about Trudi and Finn, and Finn ended up on the wrong end of a spot of jiu jitsu himself.

Grantly observed at the beginning of the episode that the school playground was like "the *Jeremy Kyle* holding pen." He had a point, you know. As well as all these muggings and beatings, we had Emily James (who's gone bad following her sister's imprisonment for killing their dad for sexually abusing her) picking up an older boy so she could snog him and nick his wallet at break time. She was only trying to cheer up Scout, who was convinced that Phoenix had another girlfriend because he kept looking at his phone. A nice bar of chocolate would have been a simpler plan.

Phoenix, whose only interesting features are his name and his hair, because he's otherwise the very definition of bland, wasn't texting another girl. Of course he wasn't. He was looking at the video of head teacher Michael Byrne wielding a stick in the general direction of the bloke who stabbed him, who got run over seconds later. Poor Michael

Byrne. He was convinced he was going to be arrested, then the car driver turned out to have been drunk so it looked like he was going to get blamed – but then this inconvenient little video was emailed to him. As a consolation, it looks like Sian Diamond is, implausibly, finding him irresistible. I know her husband has Botox and is a useless lump, but would a fabulous woman like that really look twice at weasel-faced Byrne? When there's Tom Clarkson wandering around aimlessly with his big blue eyes and his animal magnetism?

And, talking of animals, there was a silly sub plot involving Linda Radleigh's lost rabbit.

He goes the extra mile for these kids 3/11/2011

As one of our readers pointed out on Twitter last night, there really should be a race track installed around the perimeter of Waterloo Road, the number of vehicles that get nicked and driven off at high speed there.

This week it was the two-wheeled scooter thing belonging to Phoenix, and it was "borrowed" by new boy Freddie Jackson. Freddie's issue (you're not allowed to attend Waterloo Road unless you have an issue, unless you're a non-speaking extra) was that he'd had a heart transplant. It was a classic case of a boy who's been wrapped in medical cotton wool for years wanting to be "normal," so he didn't bother telling PE teacher Jez Diamond about the heart transplant till he keeled over while playing football.

It's often the case that a vehicle gets stolen when there's a visiting dignitary, and they don't come much more dignitary than the very regal Jane Asher (formerly Paul McCartney's girlfriend and Joseph Byrne's mum in *Holby*, but at different times in her career). She represented a Big Company which had the power to grant a lot of money to Waterloo Road, or not. You kind of knew the verdict would be "not," what with boys collapsing on the football field and stealing scooters, the head teacher turning into a gibbering idiot during a presentation because he's being blackmailed by one of the pupils, two girls (Scout and Emily) bobbing off for the afternoon to steal vodka and get tattoos and Finn and Trudi using the school debate to work out their personal differences. It was mesmerising stuff and could only have been improved by Ronan Burley taking to the stage to reprise his stripping routine.

Linda Radleigh turns out to be a bunny boiler of the highest order as well. Having spied Sian and Michael's secret liaison at the end of last week's episode, she's getting her revenge by dropping not-so-subtle hints about them to anyone who'll listen (mainly to Jez, and she mustn't be too subtle with Jez – he doesn't strike me as that bright), keying Michael's car and leaving him a rather pretty wreath in a box on his desk. No wonder he's all jittery. Sian told Jane Asher that Michael "Goes the extra mile for these kids" – but will the extra mile be round the bend?

Undone, by a sat nav and a Regency Hotel pen 11/11/2011

The secret love of Michael Byrne and Sian Diamond is a secret no more. Jez's suspicions were confirmed by his supposed-to-be-clever wife forgetting to erase the recent locations on the car's sat nav. When it showed that Sian had been overnighting at the Regency Hotel rather than comforting a fed-up mate, and when a Regency Hotel pen turned up on Michael Byrne's desk, Jez put two and two together and showed it's not only maths teachers who can do sums. Then he punched Michael, and PLA Jr and I cheered.

Well, he's had it coming, and he has such a punchable face. The Regency Hotel had another visitor, in the shape of Linda Radleigh, who has taken to skulking in the corridors and sending little notes to Michael. What a deeply weird woman she is. But maybe not as weird as Sian, who is Jaye Jacobs and therefore stunningly beautiful. What on earth does she see in Michael Byrne? Not much of a catch, is he?

One man who is a catch is the utterly magnificent and wonderful Ronan Burley. He's leaving soon, and I'll miss him a lot. This week he had a poor misunderstood girl throwing herself at him. It wasn't Vicki, it was another one. This was pupil-with-issues-of-the-week Andi O'Donnell. She was the daughter of a local radio presenter whose USP was talking in a cheesy voice (ok, that's not particularly U for a radio presenter) and being very confessional about her personal life and her family. This included telling all of her listeners that her 15-year-old daughter was a virgin and had never even been on a date. Andi's classmates had never twigged that Andi was this woman's daughter. Probably because they'd never seen her before this week (we'd have noticed her because of her lurid hair extensions). But when Mommy Dearest was invited to broadcast from the school as part of this week's Controversial New Initiative, Andie was humiliated in front of the whole school.

She responded by having a quick makeover, courtesy of Scout and Emily, and taking Ronan Burley out to the local park and making a grab for his trouser-front. Ronan had come to her attention after Emily and Scout had hidden her clothes during PE earlier, and he'd rushed along a crowded corridor to cover her up with his jacket. He is such a gentleman! And because he's such a gentleman, he politely declined Andie's offer of a lunchtime fumble. And he did it so beautifully as well. Andie stomped off, humiliated, and told everyone it had happened anyway.

One person who stood by Our Ronan was Vicki. She'd been in a chemistry exam while all this was going on, but she knew Ronan wasn't the type to take advantage of a vulnerable girl. That was more the style of Aiden Scotcher, as Vicki learned only too well.

Meanwhile, we thought it was too good to be true – a feisty female Muslim TV character, and no-one has even mentioned arranged marriages! How refreshing! But wait – they have. The lovely Trudi is pencilled in to marry someone called Harris. Only she doesn't want Harris, she wants Finn Sharkey. Her mad brother Tariq was mainly too busy to kick off this week, as he was helping Daniel Chalk make a pie. Tariq is this season's Michaela – one week a crazy thug, the next week playing the flute/baking a pie respectively, the next week a crazy thug again.

Meet the gang 23/2/2012

The start of yet another half term on Waterloo Road (I seem to say that with increasing regularity. Are the terms getting shorter, or is it just old age creeping up on me?). No exploding caravan or child lost on the moors for this episode. Rather than Rochdale Gothic, WR went for Inner City Gritty and we had an episode filled with dangerous gangland violence like graffiti, knife-wielding, setting fire alarms off and pouring Sprite on the teacher's desk.

It was Tariq who did the Sprite thing, and I think that tells us all we need to know about his bad boy credentials. He's not really cut out for this hard man stuff. We already knew that, of course, because we were there when Trudi was telling Finn how Tariq used to cry a lot when he was in the Young Offenders Institute. Tariq had been settling down fairly nicely in Waterloo Road, give or take the odd bout of threatening behaviour, but this week he got dragged back into the world of gangland crime by one Mason Price, a school pupil who looked older than many of the teachers and who seemed to have styled his fringe with a mascara wand. In other words, he was Hard. Every Mr Big needs a right hand man, and Mason's was Kyle Stack, who was over-compensating for his seductive body popping in the school pantomime by being all snarly and unpleasant.

When you join a gang you have to prove yourself by doing something particularly mean, and Tariq was required to beat up, and preferably stab, Finn Sharkey. Finn was a suitable target because he's going out with Tariq's sister, the lovely Trudi, and Tariq was especially disgruntled because Trudi has stopped wearing a headscarf at school. Now, this wasn't Finn's fault at all, and in fact he'd bought her a hijab for her birthday because he's Culturally Sensitive, but Tariq is not a man for subtleties like that. Anyway, it was all sorted out when Daniel Chalk turned up on a bike and Finn escaped with nothing worse than a bloody nose, which he manages to get at least once a series so it's best he got this one out of the way.

If only gangs of rampaging youths were the only worry at Waterloo Road. There was also the issue of head teacher Michael Byrne having been run over at the end of the last episode – by a member of staff, no less. He couldn't remember anything about the accident, and everyone else was blaming Jez Diamond. he had the motive, after all, what with his wife running off with the aforementioned Mr Byrne. But Jez had been with Janeece at the time, so she knew he hadn't done it.

Once again, it was Chalky to the rescue. When he confiscated some spray paint from Tariq, which had come from the boot of Linda Radleigh's car, Chalky noticed a few headmaster-shaped dents in the car bonnet. It was like CSI Rochdale.

Our Josh's descent into drugs hell 9/3/2012

Our Josh's spiral into the grip of the dreaded weed has been as sudden and unexpected as… well, as most things on Waterloo Road, really. Last week he was found to be partial to a bit of waccy baccy. This week we found he was also partial to to his dealer, one Grady. We kind of got the feeling that Grady wasn't going to be the next Nate, as he was clearly more interested in business than the pleasures of Josh. Josh ended up brokenhearted and puking all over a temporary English teacher.

There were two temporary English teachers this week. They were being interviewed for the post of Head of English. One was hippy and dippy and was full of the joys of Dickens, and the other one was a tough, no-nonsense army type. You can guess which one got the job, and it was mainly due to her hunting down and pursuing Josh's drugs dealer with the relentless guile and sheer athleticism of a jaguar or Chris Mead. I was actually thrilled to see her sprinting across the playground at the end of the episode, because I've missed having a teacher who could run.

The teacher who didn't get the job attempted to bag herself a consolation prize by asking headmaster Michael Byrne out for a drink. There is something about that head teacher chair at Waterloo Road – it renders anyone who sits in at as completely magnetic to the opposite sex. I reckon it's the pheromones left behind by Jack Rimmer.

Talking of pheromones, Trudi and Finn decided to take their relationship "to the next level." Finn stocked up on condoms, because he's a responsible citizen. He'd better stock up on full body armour when Tariq finds out. Finn and Trudi had to make a video for the school website, and Evil Kyle Stack left the camera running while they were messing about. It landed them in hot water with Sian, who thought they should take their head girl/boyship seriously, but I wonder whether some of the more incriminating footage won't find its way to Tariq.

Grantly lost £800 of his Avon lady money and it was found by Phoenix, who took Denzil and Scout on a shopping spree to buy flashy headphones and trainers – basically, anything they could find that would be blatantly obvious to anyone looking for some lost money. Think of all the drugs Josh could have bought with £800.

Our Josh's descent into mental illness 15/3/2012

Our Josh's Drugs Hell didn't last long, in the sense that he became hooked on the pernicious weed one week and was off it the next, but apparently he's consumed enough of it that he's now suffering psychotic episodes. He spent this episode twitching quietly in one corner or another. What was needed to turn a low-level bubbling anxiety into all-out panic was for a fire alarm to go off and for Josh to subsequently be appointed Fire Monitor. He started seeing danger everywhere, and ended up smashing his hand against a fire alarm and crouching under a desk, having a bit of a cry and bleeding a fair amount. "He needs a doctor," suggested Nikki Boston (with that level of insight, the Pastoral Care crown should surely be hers). Tom thought he just needed a lie down, but off to the doctor he went, and it seems Our Josh may have the beginnings of schizophrenia. Oh, Josh. I can't help thinking you wouldn't have got into this mess if you'd still had Nate and if Finn wasn't completely preoccupied with The Lovely Trudi all day long.

Meanwhile, Zack Diamond got it into his head that he wasn't a chip off the old Diamond, based on the fact that (a) he has ginger hair and his parents and sister don't (b) he likes drama and his dad likes football and (c) everyone keeps saying, "You're nothing like your dad." Including his dad. So he sold his laptop to pay for a DNA test (I can just hear Jeremy Kyle raging, "This should have been done when the kid was two weeks old, not 14!"). While the world waited with bated breath for the results, Jez realised his son was, in fact, a little Diamond in every sense of the word. The problem was, there was just a shred of doubt in his mind that maybe he wasn't, but they had a father/son bonding moment anyway, and then Jez got the call to let him know he was the daddy. Hurrah!

Matt Wilding is also a dad, of a baby who looks like an irritable 93 year old (apologies to the baby actor's parents, but I'm sure he or she will unwrinkle in time; they generally do). He didn't know he was going to love fatherhood as much as he does, but he does, so he wasn't best pleased to discover the baby's mother is now with the baby's paediatrician (are you following this?) and they were all planning to move to Bristol. It was all a fuss about nothing – no sooner had Matt had time to look gobsmacked and cry a bit than the mother of the child was promising they'd look for a job a bit nearer than Bristol and she would even dump the paediatrician if he wanted.

Trudi had forgotten it was the anniversary of her mother's death, and only had seconds to spare to throw on a headscarf and leg it down to the cemetery to join Tariq and Naseem at the graveside. We didn't hear any more about the plans she and Finn had last week to take their relationship to The Next Level, but judging by the previews for next week, I'm guessing they went ahead with the scheme, and were not entirely thorough with the bag full of condoms Finn had. Oh, Trudi.

And Grantly tried to get back the money Scout, Denzil and Phoenix spent by getting them to wash cars. All this lighthearted stuff is leading to a very sad episode next week, when Fleur's health deteriorates.

Teachers – when will they ever learn? 29/3/2012

When you go for a job as a teacher at Waterloo Road they sit you in front of the interview panel with a cup of tea and a custard cream and they ask, "What do you know about boundaries and the pupil/teacher relationship?" If you shrug your shoulders, look blank and fill the ensuing awkward silence by dunking your biscuit in your tea – you've got the job. I swear that's the only explanation for the entirely thick behaviour Jez Diamond displayed this week – has he not learned the lessons of Ms Montoya and Jonah, or Chris Mead and [insert name of just about any female pupil here]?

Guest Pupil of the Week was Mercedes, who runs as fast as the car that shares her name, at least over short distances. PE teacher and ex footballer Jez was thrilled to be able to mentor such a promising athlete, but it ended in tears when she twisted her ankle during a so-called "fun run" (those two words should never be found so close together in my opinion). Despite numerous WR pupils jogging past who could have summoned Tom Clarkson in his little red car, Jez decided the only thing for it was to help Mercedes limp back to her conveniently adjacent home. Where of course she pounced on him, and of course her brother came back and Drew Conclusions, and Jez got suspended. Mercedes is a nice girl and fessed up that she hadn't *really* been molested by the Diamond geezer, but he has to stay suspended anyway, for being a daft chump. And Sian dumped him, too.

Meanwhile, the fun run had "stirred up a hornet's nest," according to Michael, frowning as usual. "I think we might have invited a turf war into the school." Gosh, how dramatic. So far, it's been a fairly small scale turf war – basically a couple of lads squaring up to Kyle Stack and Tariq. What Jez in his football days might have called "handbags at dawn." But in a school of only 15 speaking pupils and a handful of silent extras, a lot of mayhem can be caused by handbags.

I didn't blog about Waterloo Road last week, because time sort of escaped me and it was time for the next episode before I'd managed to do it. So I'd just like to say how beautifully Philip Martin Brown and Lorraine Cheshire played the story of Fleur's death. It was genuinely moving. This week, everyone agreed he'd come back to work too soon, but it took Harley reading something he'd written about his Nan to make Grantly realise he needed to give himself time to grieve. Philip Martin Brown is a marvellous actor and the tension in his face when Harley was reading was incredible, as he tried to keep his Grumpy Grantly face from giving away how he was feeling.

Lauren wanted to know how Our Josh was feeling, because he hadn't been at school. She popped round to see him. He told her he had schizophrenia, but it was ok because he had some pills for it. He didn't *seem* unwell, Lauren observed. He agreed, and they decided he maybe didn't need those pills after all. Oh, Josh. Next week's preview would seem to indicate that coming off those pills was not a sensible plan.

Is it a sensible plan for Janeece to get married to the handyman she's known for five minutes who seems a little too insistent that he's not interested in the contents of her savings account? And when did Janeece manage to accrue savings, going as she did from party girl to single mum in one fell swoop? And is it a sensible plan for them to get married in an ice rink? This last point is obviously not sensible at all, but it is very, very Janeece. The wedding is next week and I can't wait.

And Trudi dumped Finn. It's because she doesn't want to tell him she's pregnant and is planning to not be pregnant soon. But she has told her sister, who thinks Finn has a right to know. I'm sensing one of those "desperate dash to the abortion clinic"-type scenes looming.

Our Josh's descent into A level Media Studies 6/4/2012

Poor Josh. He took some illegal medications and they rather upset him mentally, so he took some prescription medications and that helped for a while, but now he's stopped taking them and he's really, *really* upset. What you don't want when you're feeling fragile is to become darkly obsessed with the Plague – who knew it had had such an impact on Rochdale? – via the medium of the film you're making for A level Media studies. Making a no-budget Hammer horror film – slash – historical documentary in the school basement wasn't a good idea, either, as people generally only go there to have a breakdown. Poor Josh. It all led to him thinking he had the plague and scratching his arm to shreds during an exam. An ambulance was called, but to compound Josh's trouble he was unlucky enough to have non-speaking extras as paramedics, so they weren't much help.

Meanwhile, it was Janeece's wedding. Chalky had laid on a pink stretch limo for her, and practically the entire school (15 speaking pupils and a handful of silent extras) managed to hide behind it to spring out and surprise her. I was surprised that she didn't want Our Cheryl at the wedding. It's not like Janeece to miss an opportunity to deck her child out in something from the Katie Price Budget Bridesmaid Range. I was less surprised that the groom failed to show, because it was obvious from his very first appearance that that man was up to no good. It was doubly obvious last week when he kept telling her he wasn't bothered about money. To place that much emphasis on not being bothered about money can only mean you're *really* bothered about money. So while poor Janeece was at the registry office waiting for him, he was busy packing all her worldly goods into a big van. The cad. She really needs to fall for Chalky. I know he's not much to look at, but he can play the guitar, ride a bike (sort of) and he'll never pack all her worldly goods into a big van and drive them away. Quite a catch, in other words. The reception went ahead at the school, and we discovered that Janeece has no friends or relatives of her own, because there was no-one at the wedding apart from school staff and pupils.

Meanwhile, can I just say that Jack McMullen is a bloody brilliant actor? When Trudi miscarried the baby, Finn finally got to find out about the pregnancy. In times of dire need, Finn can be the most fabulous boyfriend. He was lovely with Sam and he was lovely with Trudi. And when he was on his own, he broke his heart. Bless him. In what was not Finn's happiest ever week, his new car got smashed up by Tariq and Kyle Stack, and this led Finn to a decision that he probably already regrets. He decided to join a rival gang. When we last saw him he was being beaten up in an attempt to prove his gang-worthiness. Oh, Finn. You're so much better than that.

And Jez was told he can come back to work, but he has to "Steer clear of Mercedes" (the pupil, not the cars). This will not be difficult, as she was only Guest Pupil for one week and has now vanished again.

Don't you dur say anything! 21/4/2012

Guest Pupil of this week was one Danilo Babicz. Have we had an asylum seeker at Waterloo Road before? We have now, because that was the Issue our Danilo was there to represent. Scout's no-good mother had arranged with Dan's brother that Scout would marry him so he could stay in the country. The problem was, Scout was rather fond of him and thought he felt the same about her. The rat! Luckily she had Phoenix and his mad hair to fall back on.

While Scout was wandering around Rochdale in a wedding dress, Kyle Stack was wandering around Waterloo Road being impressively evil. A security guard had been installed near the school gate, but he wasn't anywhere near as effective as the previous security guard, Tim Healy, and Kyle was able to slip into school without any bother and creep out Nikki Boston. There was a scene that was fairly mad even by Waterloo Road standards, in which Nikki Boston went to pieces during a class because of Evil Kyle Stack, and a small riot almost ensued before order was restored, military-style, by Shona and Rhona.

We finally discovered what the purpose of Trudi and Tariq's sister Naseem was. It was so she could get almost set on fire by Finn Sharkey and then rescued by Finn Sharkey, thus escalating all this gang business. To be honest I've given up trying to work out who is in what gang. Finn seems to get beaten up on a weekly basis whether he's in a gang or not and on a weekly basis I'm on the Pauseliveaction sofa yelling, "Not his face! Not his FACE!"

Fleur's ashes have barely had time to cool in the urn, and already Grantly is draping his pants on them. This was because he got together with the dinner lady – well, Grantly does like his food. I don't really want to dwell on this storyline too much because it would mean having to think about Grantly's private parts. If I did that I'd have to go and have my memory erased again.

Let's move on to the less worrying topic of Little Zack Diamond, who got fed up with being a chip off the old Diamond (it was only a couple of weeks ago he was having DNA tests and bonding with Papa like nobody's business, but that's kids for you and parents can be, like *so* embarrassing) and decided to change his name to Zack Brown. No idea why, really, but he found it hilariously easy to crack Janeece's password to the school computer to change his name on there.

At the end of the episode, a big bombshell was dropped – Waterloo Road is going to close! And, coincidentally, Michael Byrne has had the offer of a job running a school in Scotland. *Scotland*, huh? Looks like my visions of Jack Rimmer in a kilt were a bit premature.

If the crossbow doesn't get you, the delivery truck will
28/4/2012

Oh my giddy aunt. I don't even know where to start with Wednesday's Waterloo Road – the last in the term, the last in the series and the last in Rochdale. Exploding caravans? Teachers running away to marry their pupils? Mild and uneventful in comparison.

At the risk of sounding like a twisted game of Cluedo, we had Kyle Stack in the assembly hall with a crossbow. The crossbow was pointed at the (greasy – lay off the Brylcreem, lad) head of Finn Sharkey. This ghastly assassination attempt was thwarted by Our Josh, who legged it back from being suspended scarily off the edge of a multi-storey car park by pocket sized gangster Eugene ("I'm a man of deed and I follow through, you get me?" he muttered menacingly, before being scared off by Tom Clarkson and failing to follow through). "Kyle has a crossbow and it is aimed at Finn's Brylcreemed head!" shouted Our Josh (or something similar) and it was enough to put Mr Stack off his aim and Our Josh took one in the shoulder as a result.

But he survived, so phew and everything. How we all laughed and sighed with relief and waved goodbye to Evil Kyle Stack as he was apprehended by the Feds. Another school prom over, and nothing worse to show for it than a winged Our Josh and Finn sporting a black eye. This was from a previous incident – apparently I've been wasting my breath yelling "Not his FACE!" every week.

There was also a small matter of the school closing down, but Michael Byrne had a Plan. He was going to open a new school in Scotland. A school funded by Daniela Denby-Ashe off of *My Family*, who wouldn't bother with all this education authority red tape nonsense – why, they'd be free to have a Controversial New Initiative twice a week if they felt like it! And he was going to take his finest teachers and Grantly Budgen. And the dinner lady, who would be running a boarding house for pupils like Phoenix and Harley and Scout, who hadn't yet been poached for roles on *Doctors* or *Corrie* (hello, Bolton Smiley – we spotted you the other night out with That Kylie Platt). And Janeece, because she might be rubbish as a secretary, but… ok, no redeeming features as a secretary, but we love her to bits.

It was a brave step and a bold move, and you're not going to want to up sticks and go all the way to Scotland without having a look at it first, so off they popped in the school minibus. When they got to the border, Denzil wanted a photo. He'd never been abroad before, bless him. While everyone was clustered around the Welcome to Scotland sign, Grantly took the opportunity to propose to the dinner lady and everybody was so busy saying, "Aaaahhh!" and thinking, "But Fleur's only been gone five minutes!" they didn't notice a lorry leave the road and head straight for them.

And that was the end. Goodbye term. Goodbye Rochdale. Goodbye beloved cast member? We'll have to wait and see.

Out of body experience 3/9/2012 (Series 8)

I missed episode one of the new series of Waterloo Road (apart from the first 10 minutes) and decided to just dive straight in to episode two. Frankly, it was like falling down a rabbit hole.

Some of the familiar landmarks were there – Tom Clarkson, Grantly Budgen, The Adorable Josh – but we weren't in Rochdale anymore, Toto, we were within picturesque shimmering distance of the Clyde. Michael Byrne has always spoken with a Scottish accent, what with being Scottish and that, and I expected a certain amount of Scottishness, but certainly not from Jane Beale out of *EastEnders*, who's apparently an alcoholic teacher these days. She's the mother of an extremely pretty son, Connor, who may be easy on the eye in a pale-eyed, alien-type way, but is more than a tad weird. You can forgive him this, what with the alcoholic mother and everything, plus he is not the strangest kid in the school by a long chalk.

The strangest kid in the school award had to go to Problem Pupil of the Week, the Grace Jones-haired, manically-staring Lula. Turned out she wasn't mad, or bad, but her uncle thought she was possessed by demons and she'd been pencilled in for an exorcism. This never happened in Rochdale, but you can bet if it had, Tom Clarkson would have sorted it out, like he sorted out poor Lula and her predicament.

This all helped him to get over the guilt he was feeling at the loss of poor Denzil, whose enthusiasm for having his picture taken at the Scottish border had led to him being mown down by a wayward truck (which also put Tariq in a wheelchair). A memorial tree was planted and you had to feel for the absent Rose Kelly – two of her children have now become memorial trees and they're not even in the same country, never mind the same school playground.

Tom gave a rubbish eulogy, such was the depth of his guilt and grief, and sniffed the blossom of the Denzil Memorial Shrub in a moody fashion, but there wasn't much time to dwell on the sad loss of such a young life, because he had an exorcism to interrupt and fights were breaking out among various Girls With Grudges.

The whole thing is just a bit weird. "Weird," is, of course, Waterloo Road's default setting, but everything looks so different it's all a bit (more) surreal at the moment. And I haven't even mentioned the ultra-bizarre boarding house thingy, presided over by Grumpy Grantly and the dinner lady.

We need to talk about Tariq 8/9/2012

I'm getting used to the weird new setting, with its Scottish accents, Toblerone-shaped school and bizarre boarding house. This means I can now concentrate on the everyday madness that is Waterloo Road.

I have to say I'm a little concerned about Tariq. He only broke his back at the start of the summer holidays, yet a mere couple of months later he seems to have been left to fend for himself. When his wheelchair rolled off out of reach while he was in the bath, the poor lad had to haul himself out of the tub and ended up lying on the bathroom floor waiting for Grantly to break the lock and come and help him. Added to this indignity the fact that his father isn't speaking to him, his sister Trudi is in Canada with Finn (awww, bless!), the other sister is too young to understand what he's going though and the Adorable Josh thinks the way to help is to dish out motivational self-help books, and poor Tariq was feeling like he'd be better off as a memorial tree.

While taking part in kayaking trials (no lifeguards present and a shocking lack of supervision), he upended the boat and attempted to do away with himself in an icy cold loch. Luckily he was within easy worrying reach of Tom Clarkson and Michael Byrne. While Tom stood on the jetty looking tense and shouting, "Tariq!" at regular intervals, Michael Byrne dashed over on a speedboat to the rescue. Michael Byrne needed a bit of positive karma, because it had just come out that he'd apparently beaten up his own father in a callous and dreadful crime. Only it wasn't, it was a boy at the end of his tether after enduring too many years of his father beating up his mother. At least by the end of the episode Tariq had got himself a new role in life, that of Man of Peace. When the warring factions of Waterloo Road and The Rival School went head to head in an after school scrap, Tariq was on hand to separate them.

Pale And Interesting Connor was still struggling with his mother, vodka-swilling Jane Beale. She's refusing any kind of help and advice from anyone, including her colleague the pointy-faced lady, who attempted to empathise. "It must be hard bringing up a teenager on your own," she said. "What would you know?" snarled Jane Beale. She actually is Scottish, you know. At least Pale and Interesting

Connor had a bit of a diversion when he got himself a girlfriend, Georgia Taylor-lookalike Imogen.

Twisted firestarter 15/9/2012

Connor and Imogen, the James Dean and Natalie Wood of Waterloo Road, didn't have an easy week this week. There's Connor's mother (Jane Beale) for starters. Being an alcoholic is one thing – Rose Kelly was an alcoholic but she was fairly charming with it and used to smile a lot – but Jane Beale is a nasty piece of work. I'm not sure if we're supposed to believe that it's all the fault of the drink and she'd be a shining example of maternal cuddliness if she was sober, because we haven't seen her sober yet. She's perfectly horrible to Connor and was also perfectly horrible to his new girlfriend Imogen. Connor's go-to strategy for dealing with his mother seems to be arson, and this week it was a bit of fire-setting in the WR basement. Guess who put the fire out? Tom Clarkson, of course. Everybody's hero. It was Connor who got the blame, which was fair enough because he was to blame, but where's Pious Kim Campbell when we need her to (a) be on top of arson and (b) spotting a cry for help when she sees one?

But back to the star crossed lovers. Imogen had a secret which she eventually trusted Connor enough to reveal to him. She's deaf and wears hearing aids. Of course Connor didn't mind, because he thinks she's lovely, so that was alright. Imogen had a far bigger problem in the form of her mother, exercise guru to the stars (school owner Lorraine Donnegan, anyway). Not only did she have a dodgy taste in leotards, she also had a borderline dodgy fancy for schoolboys, in the form of Angus. I mean, *totes* embarrassing!

Meanwhile there was some business about Michael Byrne and his father. Sian was trying to get them reunited, but I still can't bring myself to give a hoot about Michael Byrne, so I have no idea whether she succeeded or not. I was busy looking at the comments on Twitter, where opinion seemed divided between those who thought Waterloo Road was well past its sell-by date and those who were harbouring rude thoughts about the actors who play Connor and Angus.

Looking forward to the holidays 26/10/2012

Half term, and what have we learned? I've learned that I don't find the new Scottish Waterloo Road half as much fun as the old Rochdale version. The characters I liked who made the move have been gradually shipped out (Josh, Tariq, Janeece) or have been fairly invisible (Tom). There's only good old Grantly left, and since he was part of the most ludicrous "wedding" I've ever seen on TV, I don't like Grantly as much as I used to.

This is why I haven't been blogging much about Waterloo Road this series, because if I can't say something nice, I'd rather not say anything at all. I only enjoy writing about programmes I enjoy.

One character I thought I was going to enjoy was the moody Connor. Moody is good, as far as I'm concerned, and he had those pale interesting eyes and arson habit. What's not to like? Unfortunately he also had his boring mum, Jane Beale from *EastEnders*, and her alcohol problem. The main problem with Jane Beale wasn't the alcohol, it was that she was a relentlessly nasty person. There were no different dimensions to her character at all, which obviously made life hard for Connor, but it made me care less about the whole predicament.

He had a little chance at happiness this week when the entire school shipped off to home, Barbados or Rochdale, leaving the boarding house (what a rubbish idea that was, and let's hope it gets quietly dropped now most of the Rochdale contingent are working in call centres across the country) as a tempting love nest for him and Emo Imogen. Until Jane Beale rocked up to ruin it all and Connor set fire to a classroom and Emo Imogen was caught in the ensuing explosion.

The other big drama was Michael Byrne helping his father to die. I have to admit I have no idea whether touching last words were spoken, because I had to turn the volume down on the TV every time Mr Byrne Senior was on, because the coughing was making me feel queasy. Assisting a suicide is, of course, illegal (the moral issues were presented to us via the medium of Sian Diamond and Lorraine Donnegan having a little debate about it) and when we last spotted Michael he was in a particularly grim-looking police cell. I'm afraid I really couldn't care less what happens to him. He's not a patch on Jack

Rimmer or Karen Fisher (or even Rachel Mason) so I wouldn't miss him if he was banged up and they lost the key.

Ooh, I'm sounding way too negative. Was there anything I liked about this series? Yes there was. The scenery. The way the Clyde appears to be sparkling in the sunlight in the background of any shot as soon as anyone sets foot out of the school gates is quite charming.

School report for this half term: Can do better. Much better.

The name's Barry. Barry Barry 8/1/2013

Back to school after the Christmas holidays, to be greeted by news of yet another Controversial New Initiative. Waterloo Road has acquired (via the bottomless pockets of Cockney Lorraine) a new Pupil Referral Unit, also known as A Fine Excuse For Some Proper Hard Cases.

On the subject of which… enter the Barry family. The father is in prison for armed robbery, and the mother and three kids (the beautifully named Dynasty, Kacey and Barry. Yes. Barry Barry – "so good they named him twice") are not exactly paragons of citizenship themselves. And they're from Liverpool – not that WR would be guilty of stereotyping or anything.

The Barrys settled in well to Waterloo Road. Barry started his first day by sleeping with the mother of football captain Jack MacAllister and then broadcasting the episode, which he'd handily filmed, to a meeting of the sixth form. He ended it by taking head of the PRU Nikki Boston's car and putting it up for sale on eBay. He's going to fit in just fine, and he's got that Finn Sharkey bolshy/cheeky thing going on, which helps. Younger sister Kacey is what used to be called a tomboy. Probably these days we're supposed to wonder if she has gender identity issues, because she dresses like a boy and plays football like a boy. The only people who really had issues with it were the girls who thought the new boy was rather fit – till they realised he was a she. Dynasty lives up to her name – she's all big earrings, short skirts and chewing gum. And mum is Zoe Lucker, looking like she's having a lot more fun than when she was being snooty Vanessa in *EastEnders*.

Elsewhere, Michael Byrne is due in court for helping his dad to shuffle off this mortal coil, and Sian Diamond is due to give evidence against him, because Byrne Senior hadn't mentioned to her that he actually wanted to be off the mortal coil. I'm rather hoping he gets sent dahn (I can't think of that phrase in any voice other than Phil Mitchell's), because Lorraine The Cockney has sort of promised his job to Sian and she'd wear the skirt and boots of office (think Rachel Mason and Karen Fisher) most excellently.

Emo Imogen was back at school and has been scarred for life following the fire last term. She's being quite brave about it, unlike Pale Eyed Connor, who spent the day quivering behind the front room curtains at home while Imogen bellowed at the house front from the street. Connor's mum, Jane Beale from EastEnders, admitted that she was responsible for the fire and is also admitting she's an alcoholic these days. She bonded a bit with Michael Byrne in a canteen that was so full of people eating fresh fruit, and posters about fresh fruit, that I felt I was taking part in a Derren Brown experiment.

A two car family 18/1/2013

In last week's slice of our favourite hyper-realistic school-based drama, Phoenix and Harley won £200,000 on the Lottery. A life-changing sum of money, as Noel Edmonds would call it. It certainly changed Phoenix and Harley's lives. They started riding around in a stretch limo and wearing "look at me" trainers, just to show how loaded they were. It was all a slim excuse to get rid of Phoenix, who's taken his big hair to live with his dad and invest his money and his time, in the family business. Harley, meanwhile, donated his share of the cash to good causes in Africa (bless!) and is donating his time to Waterloo Road for now.

Last week we also saw the unreal spectacle of Michael Byrne (who is not being sent dahn for hastening his father's exit from the planet) actually having fun, via the medium of paddling in the sea trying to fish out Jane Beale's course outlines. That's *course*, not coarse.

There wasn't much action from the Barry family at all last week, but this week the focus shifted to Dynasty Barry and her future as a pole dancer. But she can't even speak Polish! I hear you cry. Maybe not, but she is very, very good at English Literature and produced an A* essay. Obviously wasted on the world of sleazy clubs and breast enhancements, but it took quite a lot of effort from Emo Imogen and the teacher with the little face to persuade her of the fact. It took even more effort to persuade Ma Barry. Beautiful work from Zoe Lucker as Carol Barry, who does common-as-muck like she was born to it.

Barry Barry, meanwhile, was adding to his extensive stolen car collection by "obtaining" Cockney Lorraine's Ferrari, with a little help from sister Kacey. Lorraine isn't pointing the finger at Barry, though, because Nikki Boston firmly believes that Scout is the one who stole her car a couple of weeks ago, and therefore Scout is in the frame for the Ferrari as well.

Nikki Boston's treatment of Scout contravenes all sorts of rules and regulations. Basically, she's a bully. Tom Clarkson, a man whose depth of human understanding is even deeper than the deep, deep blue of his eyes, has an inkling that Scout is being victimised. He gave her a little voice recorder so she can record her lessons and play them back in her own good time (she daren't ask Nikki Boston to repeat herself), and this will no doubt come in handy as evidence at some point.

Emo Imogen and Pale-Eyed Connor eventually made up, after she'd been made up by Dynasty Barry. A bit of blusher did wonders for her, and a pep talk from Kevin did wonders for Connor. I wish Dynasty would turn her style eye on Connor, though. That boy needs a haircut badly.

His mother probably hasn't noticed, because now she isn't spending all her time hiding bottles of vodka in desk drawers she has time for romance. With Michael Byrne, no less. Poor Jane Beale.

The mystery man and the mystery ingredient 1/2/2013

This week, Kevin found some documents on Chalky's laptop (which he'd "borrowed" to work on his award-winning robot design), which led him to suspect that Chalky might have had a previous life as a child molester. It turned out, after a lot of rushing around corridors and anguishing, that Chalky was a victim rather than a villain. This was Kevin's cue to start talking like a self-help manual (Kevin talks like a 55 year-old chartered accountant at the best of times) and get Chalky to testify in court. And – heartwarming, this – Kevin wants to change his surname to Chalk.

Emo Imogen, meanwhile, told Connor that he must tell the truth about starting the fire, or she would do it for him. Emo Imogen is seriously grating on me – her whinging voice, her miserable face. Ugh. When Michael Byrne heard that it was Connor and not Jane Beale who'd started the fire, he decided to give him a chance to stay at Waterloo Road by getting him to fess up in front of the school (several regular characters and three rows of folding seats containing non-speaking extras). Then the police took him away.

The non-speaking extras may not have been speaking, but they were all laughing. Not because they're a heartless bunch who didn't feel Connor's and Imogen's pain, but because they were all stoned. The delicious brownies that Sonya had made in honour of the visit of TV's Austin Healey (he was there to present the prize for the best robot. As PLA Jr remarked, "In the real world all you'd get would be a photocopied certificate") had an added ingredient, courtesy of Barry Barry.

In other words, just your average day at Waterloo Road.

Barry Barry's got Bolton's gun! 8/2/2013

Thank heavens for the Barry family. They might be a tad over-the-top and cartoonish, but they're funny and watchable and the three of them (Carl Au, Abby Mavers and Brogan Ellis) are all excellent actors. The Barrys are making Waterloo Road watchable because, let's face it, the rest of the permanent characters are a bit lacking in oomph at the moment. There's drippy Connor and Emo Imogen, who do nothing but look pale-faced and miserable for an hour and sometimes get together and sometimes split up – I don't particularly care which. I liked Connor a lot better when he was starting fires, but he's put his pyromaniac career aside for now. Out of the other pupils, Scout and Kevin are semi-interesting, but that's it.

I miss the likes of Ronan Burley, Finn and Josh, Lauren and Amy, Sam Kelly, Chlo and Donte, Michaela, Janeece etc etc. So naturally I was very happy to see Bolton Smiley (Tachia Newall) pitch up this week. Tom Clarkson was also happy to see Bolton, looking Action Man-smart in his army uniform and just back from Afghanistan. Everybody said how proud they were that Bolton was doing his bit for his country, apart from Grantly Budgen, who muttered about "cannon fodder" and quoted Wilfred Owen.

It didn't occur to anyone to wonder why a boy who'd gone to school in Rochdale would pitch up at a school he'd never seen before in Scotland to look up his old teachers – of which there were only two, and one of those didn't like him. When he started having flashbacks about Afghanistan and Barry Barry found a gun in Bolton's backpack, it was only a matter of time before there'd be a "He's got a GUN!" stand-off in a classroom and non-speaking extras hurtling for the exits in blind panic. The day was saved by Grantly Budgen's calmness, and throughout the episode the scenes between Grantly and Bolton were real and believable.

Elsewhere, Dynasty Barry was cross that Connor was still hanging around upsetting her new mate Emo Imogen. She and Kacey decided to give Connor a punishment fitting his crime and burn him. Well, singe him a bit. Seeing her pale-faced ex-boyfriend in peril was enough to send Imogen rushing to his aid and back into his arms against a suitably miserable backdrop of a derelict block of flats. If only they could be fun goths, like Rosie and Craig used to be in *Corrie*.

At least three people not pregnant 15/2/2013

By the end of the episode we'd established that three people weren't pregnant. Emo Imogen wasn't (can you imagine Connor's sperm having the energy? He looks like he can barely blink without having a lie down afterwards). Jane Beale wasn't, because Michael Byrne had "been careful" (don't make me imagine that – I'd have to have my brain wiped), and Jade wasn't because she'd just given birth five minutes before the episode ended.

She gave her baby to a woman who hardly ever blinked (welcome to Connor's world), who would give her a better start in life. The alternative for the poor child was too ghastly to contemplate. It would have been grandmother-smothered by dreadful dinner lady Maggie, who was being ridiculously manipulative and emotionally blackmailing in trying to get Jade to keep the baby. And it would have had a fine succession of "aunties and uncles" of the likes of Scout, Harley and Rhiannon – who at least were more realistic than Maggie about the downsides to having a baby on the premises.

Obviously Jade went into labour at school, but as luck would have it for the five minutes while she waited for the ambulance, the school population had apparently vanished. She was left with Grantly Budgen as the only adult representative. He sent for hot water and towels (why?) but didn't think of sending for the school nurse, who we know exists because she was used as an excuse earlier when Jade went AWOL, or for Sian Diamond or the all-purpose Tom Clarkson.

Nikki Boston had organised a presentation so the pupils of the PRU could showcase their skills and show Lorraine "Too Cockney To Function" Donnegan that her money was being well spent. It seems it certainly is. Jade expressed herself via the medium of rap just before the contractions kicked in; Connor gave a presentation on Steampunk (no idea why); and Barry Barry depicted some of the key staff members via the medium of caricature. Frankly Tom Clarkson's face was just made to be a cartoon, those big blue eyes always trembling on the edge of tears. But it's Ms Diamond that Barry Barry seems to have taken a shine to. He probably remembers when she was The Radiant Donna in *Holby*. Anyway, he seems to have become quite attached to her, in a way that threatens to turn ever so slightly Jonah Kirby/Ms Montoya on us.

And Connor and Emo Imogen are engaged. This would be heartwarming, if PLA Jr and I didn't keep doing impressions of Connor saying "I burned Imogen!" (in a voice that conveys all the emotion of "I mislaid a sock, but I'm confident it'll turn up") every time his face appears on the screen. I know – we need to grow up.

We can be winners – just for one night 23/2/2013

Thanks to the goal-scoring skills of star player Kacey Barry, Waterloo Road were in the final of the Unspecified Cup. Hurrah! But the problem was, FA rules (or some official rules somewhere) stated that girls couldn't play in boys' teams once they were over 15, in case they broke a nail or terrorised the boys with a mascara wand.

These things were not likely to be a problem with Kacey Barry – a less girly-girl you couldn't wish to meet. But it went further than that – Kacey actually feels that she *is* a boy, with an unfortunately female body. So she was gutted to hear she wouldn't be playing in the cup final. Tom Clarkson was gutted, as well. He knew the team had no chance of winning without Kacey. His team just didn't have what Alan Hansen would call "strength in depth." Being a man (or woman) down, they even had to resort to Connor – who'd never played anything more physical than mah jong in his life – going in goal.

There was only one thing for it. Kacey would play and everyone would pretend she was a boy and everything would be lovely, and Michael Byrne would forget to be angry with Tom Clarkson because he'd be so thrilled that Waterloo Road had actually won something. It would have worked, too, if a girl Kacey had befriended earlier hadn't kissed her on the lips when she scored the winning goal. This kind of behaviour is not the sort of thing that Barry Barry wants to see happening with his sisters, and he he said so. Loudly. There were gasps of horror, Tom Clarkson got suspended and Waterloo Road are going to be stripped of their win – though Tom Clarkson told Michael Byrne he'd let them enjoy the victory for a while before he told them.

Meanwhile, Barry and his younger sister were having a heart-to-heart, Barry-style, about her gender issues. This involved Kacey saying she'd always felt like a boy and Barry attempting to change her mind by covering her in makeup in a locked classroom. This was a really shocking and disturbing scene, not least because Barry is no Francois Nars with the blusher brush.

I'm a bit worried about Barry, actually. He seems to be slipping from cheeky bad boy to sinister bad boy, and I don't like it. Last week he seemed to be developing a bit of a crush on The Radiant Sian (and who can blame him?). This week they had a bit of a show-down and he was rather scary. At the end of the episode he followed her home and stood outside looking threatening. This is not what I want from Barry, who I think needs to occupy more the Finn Sharkey end of the Finn Sharkey/Kyle Stack continuum.

While all this was going on, Connor and Emo Imogen started and ended the episode smiling – honestly, they did. In the middle they had a falling-out because she wouldn't wear her engagement ring in public. She made it up to him by fashioning an amulet for him, made of the congealed tears of baby dragons and the fingernails of ancient shepherds. Scout helped. Connor loved it. And they even had time to do some matchmaking between Jane Beale and Michael Byrne, because miserable people in love always want other miserable people to be in love too.

You can't go slapping Barry Barry 1/3/2013

I tweeted earlier this week that whoever thought of Barry Barry's name was a genius. It's memorable, it's funny and it instantly labels him as Somebody. It describes him and defines him – everything he does is about not only living up to being A Barry, it's about living up to being *The* Barry.

So when Sian went against him in supporting Kacey about her gender issues, Barry just couldn't let it go. She'd also insulted his male ego by calling him a boy, so his revenge had a sexual element. Actually, it could have been a lot worse – he broke into her flat and managed to creep around fairly easily while she was in her underwear and in the shower – but Barry Barry isn't evil and he has his own moral code, so all he did was to steal a photograph of Sian and Michael Byrne kissing, and a pair of her knickers.

After that it was a simple matter of taunting her – which Barry does most effectively. Because she wouldn't be working at Waterloo Road if she had anything resembling teaching skills, she handled the sudden appearance of the photo all around the school all wrong by trying to humiliate him in a sex ed class, but it was Sian who ended up getting most wound up and she slapped him. Hard.

That's the sort of thing that'll get you dismissed, although Kacey and the other class members did their best to protect Sian with the old "I'm Spartacus" routine, each of them saying they'd slapped Barry (as if they'd dare). It was no use – Sian resigned, because she'd slapped Barry, or because she realised she still had unprofessionally cuddly feelings for Michael Byrne, or a mixture of both. It was really sad to see her go, because Jaye Jacobs is lovely and because she always will be The Radiant Donna from *Holby* as far as I'm concerned. Before she left she got the Barry family to at least start to accept Kacey's gender agenda before she left, just to underline what a loss she'll be to the school. The entire weight of pastoral care has now fallen back on the shoulders of poor Tom Clarkson, who looks more tearful every week.

Elsewhere, there was a ludicrous story involving a mobile phone game that Kevin and Chalky had devised, that despite looking like a poor version of Pac Man was so darned addictive that everyone in the school was playing it. Cockney Lorraine spotted a money-making opportunity and before you could say "Duncan Bannatyne wants to drill down into the details" she'd made Kevin an offer he couldn't refuse.

Jane Beale found out about Pale Connor and Emo Imogen being engaged. She wasn't thrilled – there's enough misery in her life already, without losing a son and gaining an emo. So in the face of opposition the whey-faced couple have decided to get married straight away. And Scout's useless mother turned up and wasted no time in getting drunk and being parked in a spare room at the school boarding house. That's not going to end well.

A wedding, a death, a serious illness and a job offer
8/3/2013

What did I love about this episode? Against expectations, I loved the wedding – particularly the part when Connor busted out his sign language moves. I'd completely forgotten that Imogen is deaf (or partly deaf), so it was unexpected but completely appropriate, touching and beautiful. It even made Emo Imogen genuinely smile.

I also loved the acting of Katie McGlynn as Jodie/Scout. Her useless mother died, and Jodie's reaction was to go straight to school to sit her exam, so she could get a place at university and become a teacher and try to inspire and support kids the way the Waterloo Road staff have inspired and supported her over the years. I know – snarf at that last bit, since she spent most of this term being bullied by Nikki Boston. But we'll forget all that for the sake of a happy ending for Scout, as we see her leave Waterloo Road for the bright lights of university. Or *Coronation Street*.

There wasn't all that much Barry action in this episode, but there were two nice little scenes involving Kacey. In one, Tom Clarkson caught her reading some leaflets during class and was about to tell her off, but when he saw they were about her gender issues he covered neatly and she gave him a silent little 'thank you.' In the other, Kacey was trying to persuade Barry to accept her, and he said something like, "You don't even know who you are," and she said, with a look of quiet determination, that she *did* know who she was. I do love the Barrys and I'm looking forward to seeing how Kacey's story moves on.

So what did I not love about the episode? Some of the dialogue was dreadful. Most of those kids don't talk like any teenager I've ever met (and the teenager I live with agrees with me). It's not just the kids, either. The IT expert who appeared from Down London to offer Daniel Chalk a job on the basis of his 'addictive' mobile phone game would have been funny if it was an episode of The Office, but in this he was just painful. Any scene Cockney Lorraine appears in is generally awful, though I did enjoy the little frisson between her and Nikki Boston (anyone remember Daniela Denby-Ashe's foxy turn in *Torchwood*?).

As a student of the *Holby* school of televisual medicine, I was a bit disturbed by the hospital's somewhat rubbish attempt to do CPR on

Scout's mother. They didn't even lie her flat! Since Grantly Budgen is currently in (presumably) the same hospital awaiting a kidney transplant (years of unchecked high blood pressure, apparently) I have to say I'm worried about the standard of care he can expect to receive. That pillowcase on its own would sap my will to live.

And Scout was finishing her exam at 4.30 (there was a very big clock on the wall), but all the pupils were shown leaving school some time later. Does the school day finish a lot later in Scotland? Or does Cockney Lorraine get to decide on the timings of the school day?

This and other troubling questions will have to wait until the next series, in which there'll once again be a languages department (there's been nothing since the last languages teacher tried to run off with a pupil), with the arrival of Angus Deayton.

The return of the giant broccoli 5/5/2013

Back we go to Waterloo Road, refreshed after the holidays. Sian Diamond has gone, and Cockney Lorraine has replaced her as Deputy Head with girlfriend Nikki Boston. It is her school, after all, so she doesn't have to go through boring stuff like a proper recruitment procedure. Though Lorraine's accountant has spotted that there's not a lot of money to be made in a school (unless you're Barry Barry and have sidelines in drugs and nicked cars) and has advised her to dump it. Lorraine, however, isn't just in it for the money. She has a Vision, and like Michael Byrne she wants to do her best for the people they both insist on referring to as "These Kids." If it comes down to a contest between These Kids and her Ferrari, though, she's going to have a tough decision on her hands.

Grantly Budgen needs a new kidney, and Maggie the Dinner Lady isn't a suitable match. He is therefore currently undergoing regular dialysis at home, which is the front bedroom of the boarding house for troublesome teens. As if the troublesome teens don't have enough to worry about already.

The thing worrying Connor and Emo Imogen is how Jane Beale is going to take the news that they're already married. They weren't the *most* worried pupils this week, though. That would be problem-pupil-of-the-week Fergal Doherty, pursued by the father of his ex girlfriend who died of something drugs-related, and making ends meet by getting Harley off his head on something potent and unspecified. Dear, innocent Harley was only saved from a long drop off the school roof by the swift intervention of someone the teacher with the pointy face picked up in Africa.

Kacey Barry, meanwhile, has decided she wants to be called Robbie ("Robbie Barry" has a certain swagger to it, I agree) and use the boys' toilets. Barry's not happy about this, and Tom Clarkson has suggested the unisex teachers' toilets as a compromise. I'm not sure who the unisex teachers are, but it's kind of them to let Robbie/Kacey use their toilets.

The most exciting thing for me this week was spotting that there's a giant sculpture of broccoli (and other veg) above the canteen door. It was only glimpsed briefly, but from now on I'm going to be on broccoli-watch to see if it reappears again. It would have gone so nicely with the W of pie from Series 6.

30% cuts week 10/5/2013

Lorraine Donnegan's accountant has told her she needs to slash the Waterloo Road budget by 30%. That's a lot of slashing, so she decided she'd start by moving into Michael Byrne's office. Has it suddenly become much larger? I'd swear it used to be a bit more snug, but maybe he used to have a false wall in there to make it smaller so Sian Diamond would have to wriggle past him for staff meetings. Now he's on a pipe-and-slippers domestic footing with Jane Beale, he has no need of such stratagems and the extra space has come in handy for Cockney Lorraine and her ergonomic desk chair.

Further savings were to be found by making Michael do an honest day's teaching instead of slumping over his desk all day waiting for disasters to happen. To make sure he could still hack it on the shop floor, Nikki Boston was dispatched to watch. If Nikki observed all the teachers, Lorraine (dress code: leather and black lace) reasoned, she'd be able to spot teachers who were not adding value, who could then be Drastically Cut.

The prime candidate for that sort of thing would in normal times have been Grantly Budgen, a man with such a gift for teaching he makes Steph Haydock look like *Dead Poets Society*. But these are not normal times for Grantly, what with having rapidly deteriorating kidneys and that. It's put a dreadful burden on Maggie the Dinnerlady, who was faced this week with the added pressure that Lorraine wanted to slash the canteen budget as well and made Maggie compete with local takeaway owner The Prince of Spices for the honour of serving the school meals.

The tiresome Verruca Salt, who had her eye on the son of the Prince of Spices (a Scottish version of Tamwar from *EastEnders*), messed Maggie around by nicking her spreadsheet and giving it to the PoS so he could undercut her figures. Dastardly! Poor Maggie, she was so disheartened by this point that she was even reduced to going to the staff room to ask around whether anyone had a spare kidney they were willing to give Grantly. Tom Clarkson looked like he might be tempted, and I wondered whether his exit storyline might be that he dies on the operating table while donating one of his vital organs to his old colleague and shop steward. It would be a fitting end for a man whose default setting is Tearful.

But let's not get ahead of ourselves. What were the Barrys up to while all this was going on? Barry Barry, who always looks like he's ready to start snapping his fingers and going into a dance routine from *West Side Story*, spent 50% of his time rolling his eyes in the general direction of his sister/brother Kacey/Robbie, and 50% entering into some kind of car financing deal with Pale Connor. Michael Byrne doesn't think it's right that Emo Imogen stays under the same roof as Connor overnight (he doesn't know they're married), so Connor had the sensible idea of getting a camper van they could use as a little bolt-hole on wheels, if only he could afford such a thing. The fact that the vehicle Barry "sourced" was a truck with no roof on the back didn't dim Imogen's enthusiasm for it. Possibly they can pitch a little wigwam on the back part.

In other news, the teacher with the pointy face's African boyfriend has apparently been given a general handyman role. Not even a whiff of a CRB check, either. Sonya "Slightly Less Cockney" Donnegan has her eye on him, but he only has eyes for the teacher with the pointy face. Sonya was showing him around the school, and pointed out the computer room. She didn't think he'd have that sort of thing where he came from. "I'm from Malawi," he said, "Not the Stone Age." That's her told.

So now to the shock finale. Maggie the Dinnerlady, having made up with Verruca Salt and won the catering contract back again, snuggled up with Grantly as he settled in for another night of at-home dialysis. We saw him smiling contentedly, but she was looking worried. Then we saw her waking up suddenly, discovering an apparently lifeless Grantly next to her, and then he was rushed off in an ambulance. Is Grantly dead? Is it too late for Tom to donate a kidney and die a hero? The little preview of next week's episode was no help, as it all seemed to revolve around Dynasty Barry proving she's a hot-shot at chess and a mysterious "Steve-O" turning up. I bet Steve-O isn't a hot-shot at chess. He looked like Trouble to me.

The future is digital 17/5/2013

It was episode 2 in Dynasty Barry's tussle between Education and Upbringing (episode one being the one where she chose education over pole dancing). With the arrival of her jailbird boyfriend Steve-O (he should wear brighter shirts then we could call him Hawaii Steve-O), all thoughts of the inter-school chess championship were thrown out of the window in favour of an engagement ring from the Katie Price for Argos Collection and a quick fumble in the Music Room.

She should have realised Steve-O was a bad sort, aside from the fact that he'd just got out of prison. She really ought to have recognised him as the nasty man who pimped out poor Whitney on *EastEnders*. Not that the actor (Jody Latham) is getting typecast or anything.

She saw the light when she saw the contents of his car boot – several top-of-the-range generic laptops which Cockney Lorraine had purchased for the school's exciting new IT facility. Steve-O was dumped, and Dynasty ended up having a Thomas Crown Affair-style erotically charged chess game with Kevin Chalk (some sterling work by Dynasty's false eyelashes), followed by a snog with him against a picturesque maritime backdrop. Talk about the odd couple… Anyhoo, Steve-O isn't going to give up that easily, and administered a kicking to Young Master Chalk as a bit of a warning to Keep Off His Bird.

Back to those laptops. Visionary Lorraine "Gor Blimey Mary Poppins" Donnegan decided this week that the way forward for Waterloo Road, educationally speaking, was to abandon all the tedious stuff like English, History, Geography, blah blah blah. IT was where it was at. You'd never get a good job doing your boring standard subjects, she informed the massed ranks of speaking and non-speaking pupils. So she had her sister and the boyfriend of the teacher with the pointy face install about a dozen laptops (give or take the ones Steve-O took and Dynasty gave back). Well, bless. The looks on the faces of those kids when they stepped in that IT room. They looked beyond excited and couldn't wait to rush to a computer and have a look for themselves, chatting excitedly. "Look! It shines with a secret inner light! Truly this is a thing from the future come to visit us in our humble school!"

With all that excitement, it was a hard task for the teachers of more conventional subjects to make them entertaining, but the teacher with the pointy face somehow managed it by brandishing a pointy sword, which she claimed to have found in a forest. This had the effect of making Harley come over all giddy with historical excitement. "That was brilliant, Miss," he gushed. "I can't believe I'd enjoy history so much."

That would have been prime contender for Cringey Dialogue of the Week, but that award goes to this gem. Jane Beale assured Maggie the Dinnerlady that Grantly, currently in a coma in a nearby hospital, was in the best hands. "He needs more than the best hands now," said Maggie. "He needs a kidney transplant." Sorry, but LOL. As I predicted last week, Tom Clarkson has volunteered himself for the aforementioned organ donation. A quick glance at a *Racing Post* was enough to convince him of what would be lost if Grantly was to die. Maggie, of course, was thrilled and relieved at this news, though the chances that Tom's kidneys will be a match for Grantly are very slim indeed. About as slim at Dynasty Barry finding Kevin Chalk attractive. Oh.

Back to the Barrys, and I was severely disappointed by Barry's behaviour this week. When the nasty Steve-O basically sexually assaulted Kacey/Robbie in an effort to find out whether s/he was male or female in the pants area, Barry stood by and did nothing to help her. I'm also rather disappointed by Kacey's later decision not to be Robbie any more. Apparently it was just a bit of a phase, and Tom Clarkson's promise of a girls' football team has been enough to persuade her that she's female after all. Now, while I'm not disputing that a lot of people do go through such a phase and then decide they were happy the way they were, there are also a lot of people for whom it isn't a phase. Waterloo Road seemed to go to a lot of effort to take the story of Kacey's gender issues seriously. Brogan Ellis's performance was brave and convincing, and the reactions of people around her (particularly Barry) and her reactions to their reactions (trying to live up to Barry as the only male role model she has) were well done. Abandoning it seems like a cop-out.

Kevin Chalk, sword of vengeance 7/6/2013

Having been without a functioning TV aerial and with internet powered by three candles and an empty baked beans can, I've been unable to watch Waterloo Road for a couple of weeks. This week I acquired an extra candle and managed to watch it on iPlayer and I'm very pleased I did. Talk about drama!

Any episode of anything that starts of with Gang of Four as a soundtrack ('Anthrax,' no less) is going to make me happy, and in this case it was the soundtrack to the dastardly "Hawaii" Steve-O outlining his plans to turn Connor's hand to burglary and other money-making crimes. If Connor hadn't already been the palest colour it's possible for a live human to be, he'd have gone pale.

The extent of Steve-O's nastiness only became clear (to me, as presumably this was seen in a previous episode) when Dynasty admitted to Kevin that he'd raped her. At this point I have to say the acting from Abby Mavers throughout this episode was brilliant, and she also has the most beautiful accent. Anyway, her admission turned Kevin into a quivering bundle of rage and he concocted a plan to kill Steve-O, with the help of Connor. This sounded about as good a plan as the one to get Connor to rob houses.

You'd think, wouldn't you, that the person who'd be the best angel of retribution in this case would be Barry Barry, who'd surely want to sort out the scum who wronged his sister. Barry's moral position is always quite marvellously ambiguous, though. When you remember how he stood by when Steve-O assaulted Kacey, and how he's more often the enabler and supplier of other people's crimes rather than the active participant, I did wonder whether he'd come through. Eventually, he did, turning up in the deserted warehouse (there's always one handy when you need one) where he'd arranged for Kevin and Connor to find a gun and shoot Steve-O (only Steve-O got the gun, which luckily Barry had neglected to load). The police turned up and Steve-O was taken away. Hurrah!

Meanwhile, the glorious Daniela Nardini has joined the cast as a science teacher, but she seems to be more interested in stirring up political unrest among the pupils by encouraging Lula to take direct action against a pharmaceutical company that Cockney Lorraine is involved with which does animal testing. This was a classic piece of

Waterloo Road bonkers-ness, with a mass demonstration of four people (Lula, Kacey, Jack and Harley), Lula managing to graffiti the word SHA onto a garage door (she had no time to add the ME) and spending lesson time composing death threats with cut-up newspaper and Pritt.

Cockney Lorraine (dress code: tartan pencil skirt)'s latest money saving initiative is that she wants the school to become fee paying. How soon they lose their ideals, eh? It was only mere weeks ago that she was importing bus-loads of Rochdale's more underprivileged citizens and setting them up in a boarding house, she was that caring. Understandably the whole scheme has upset Michael Byrne to the extent that he's resigned. He's packed up the traditional box of stuff from his desk (though unusually it didn't include a picture frame or a house plant) and he's leaving, without even mentioning it to Jane Beale first. Lorraine has promoted Nikki Boston to the head teacher role, so we can expect exercise drills at dawn in the parade ground, low-level bullying and a wider variety of unpleasant suits.

In other news, the teacher with the pointy face had a tricky time trying to stir up interest in her forthcoming marriage to her African toy-boy, because no-one quite believes it's the meeting of true minds that she thinks it is. And, sadly, they're right. It turns out he's only after a visa (surely not!) and is planning to have Less Cockney Sonya as his bit on the side once he's got the marriage certificate safely in his pocket. The rat!

An almost wedding and a sort-of strike 14/6/2013

I'm loving Waterloo Road at the moment. It's gloriously barmy, operating in an alternative universe where the real world has practically ceased to exist and only soap rules apply.

This week it was the wedding of the teacher with the pointy face and her boyfriend, who only arrived in this country from Malawi a few short weeks ago and has now been installed in the Waterloo Road basement with an *Addams Family* chair and various swooning females for company. And he has his own Waterloo Road polo shirt. No one else has one, so it must have been specially made for him.

If only he'd been specially made for Audrey, but no sooner had he set foot in his new basement than he was setting other parts of himself (don't dwell) on Less Cockney Sonya. So smitten was Sonya that she was even decorating Audrey and Ndale's wedding cake with the words "Congratulations Ndale and Sonya." It was the finest wedding cake moment since Ruby Fry smashed up Rachel Mason's cake back in Series 5.

Would she be the one standing up at the wedding at the moment the vicar asked if anyone knew any just impediment etc, shouting, "It's me he loves! Me, I tell you!"? Well, no, because she'd already made a bigger discovery. Ndale was married already! Gasp. It turned out that his plan was just to use Audrey to get himself a visa, and then bring Mrs Ndale and the kids over from Malawi once he was settled with a job Down London. I can't help thinking his scheme was not exactly watertight, but still. Audrey was left down but not beaten (can't let the buffet go to waste!), Sonya was left down but forgiven, and Ndale was left in the hands of the police, on his way to being deported but pleased that he was about to see Mrs Ndale and the kids again.

As if this wasn't enough fun for one episode, the teachers went on strike in protest against Cockney Lorraine (dress code: ankle boots)'s plan to make Waterloo Road fee-paying. It was Nikki Boston's first day in the head teacher's chair, so it wasn't ideal that she had to contend with an army of supply teachers, who were mainly non-speaking extras so therefore quite easy to handle, apart from the superbly sarcastic and snappy Angus Deayton ("When the bell goes, I go"). Where were Nikki's legendary army skills when she needed them? AWOL, that's where. Frankly, she was rubbish and she knew it and resigned. Cockney Lorraine immediately offered Michael Byrne his old job back.

He, meanwhile, had been busily plotting a council coup. In a dangerous move, he plans to have Waterloo Road taken under the wing of the local authority to become – controversial, this – a normal school. He'll have yet another fight on his hands, as Lorraine is planning to turn it into the Lorraine Donnegan Institute of Excellence – or L-DIE. She's not thought that acronym through.

As well as Angus Deayton, the other newish teacher is Esther Fairclough, who spends her time grooming Lula for a life of militant activism. Between them they're hatching a plan to infiltrate the dastardly, noxious Nox factory and cause some kind of mayhem, last week's graffiti and death threats not having been quite enough. Angus Deayton attempted to tell Lula why animal testing might just have some benefits, but she got all hissy and threw a chair at him.

Dynasty Barry is moving in with Kevin Chalk, and Barry Barry is not pleased. He beat Master Chalk up a bit, which is becoming a regular occurrence for young Kev and he might want to consider martial arts lessons. But that looks like the least of his problems, as next week Carol Barry turns up. Hurrah! Carol, hardest of all the Barrys.

Maddest ever episode. And it's not even the end of term
21/6/2013

There was rather an end-of-term feel to this episode, what with the inspirational speeches, the mass staff resignations, the change of head teacher and the thwarted acid attack. But there are still a couple of episodes of madness to go before we can hang up our lab coats and bin our pencil cases for this series.

Michael Byrne was seeking to get the local council to take over Waterloo Road from right under the nose of Cockney Lorraine, who was determined to turn the school into the fee-paying Lorraine Donnegan Institute of Excellence (L-DIE). This was the episode where Lorraine (dress code: Bible black) went completely power-crazed and was practically twirling an invisible moustache, so determined was she to get Scotland's most surreal school on a profit-making footing and bask in glory and cash. Any teacher who didn't agree with her Vision of the Future was welcome to collect their P45, she announced. Maggie the Dinnerlady said she'd stay, what with having Grantly to look after and that, but Lorraine didn't want her. Frankly Maggie's approach to power dressing would have entirely downgraded the promotional brochure and Lorraine wasn't having any of that kind of thing. The teachers with integrity (practically all of them, given that they were drawn to Waterloo Road by the prospect of Helping These Kids) all said they'd leave.

Luckily, in the opposing corner to Lozza was Michael Byrne, looking as sorrowful as ever and reminding Lorraine that before she was International Businesswoman of the Century she'd been almost as rough as Dynasty Barry. Eventually the council decided they'd take on the school, and they wanted Jane Beale to be head teacher. She is, of course, the perfect choice. She may be a just-barely-recovering alcoholic who only a few weeks ago was too pissed to remember who wrote *Pride and Prejudice* and who spent her down-time battering her pale son, but at least we know about all that and there won't be any nasty Rachel Mason-type secrets waiting to crawl out of the woodwork. The assembled seven speaking pupils and a dozen non-speaking extras heard the announcement of Michael Byrne leaving with some consternation. "Stay!" squeaked one. "Don't go!" moaned another. "You're the best head teacher ever in the history of the civilised world!" There was a small outbreak of mass-chanting and standing ovations. "Nobody likes their head teacher *that* much," muttered PLA Jr in disgust.

Meanwhile, Daniela Nardini has been shamefully under-used as Esther, the animal rights activist science teacher whose master plan consisted of inspiring Lula to acts of random and ineffective sabotage. Lula's latest plan was to throw acid at Lorraine Donnegan, but Esther guessed what she was up to and intercepted the attack, getting a nasty burn on her hand for her trouble and then getting arrested.

Carol Barry turned up to try to persuade Dynasty that she'd be better off living at Barry Towers than with Master Kevin Chalk. Dynasty disagrees, so Carol has turned to the highest power in the country – Julian Noble. Who he? Well, basically Jeremy Kyle by the sound of things. The Barry dirty laundry is due to be aired via the medium of daytime TV next week. Can't wait.

Noble Thoughts, good intentions and a miracle 27/6/2013

It's a new dawn, it's a new day, it's a new head teacher. Time to knuckle down and get those all-important qualifications, yes?

Of course not. The start of the Christine Mulgrew Era, despite the loss of Cockney Lorraine and her ever-changing dress codes and the loss of Michael Byrne and his miserable face, was as mad as a box of frogs.

Carol Barry, unhappy that elder daughter Dynasty has plumped for a life of book learnin' and domestic bliss with junior mobile app magnate Kevin Chalk, phoned up a fictional version of Jeremy Kyle to volunteer to air the Barry laundry on daytime TV. I can't help thinking that if only Dynasty had mentioned the Chalk App Millions, Carol would have been rather more well disposed towards young Kevin and would have been off sourcing a fascinator from a store with lightish security in preparation for the wedding.

Barry Barry, ever one for a money-making opportunity himself, laid on a mini bus to take half the school to join the audience of *Noble Thoughts*. We'll leave the issue of the TV studio's lax door policy to one side (teachers just bobbing in and out practically at will) and focus on the show itself, which would have had Ofcom in uproar and the Daily Mail self-combusting. Kevin thought he was there to help Dynasty confront her issues with her mother, but the show was angled at him being a nasty little family-wrecker, and just to underline how dreadful he was, they'd dredged up his own horrible mother to tell everyone what a monster he really was. The point of this was to make Carol look like a paragon of maternal virtue, which she succeeded in doing stylishly by punching Kevin's mother on stage. Kevin was embraced into the Barry family bosom and was invited for tea. Everyone bonded around a feast of Generic Fried Chicken.

You'd think Christine would have had an easy day of it back at Waterloo Road, what with the majority of her speaking pupils going AWOL for the day to the TV studio. But she had to contend with Nikki Boston being all snippy and undermining and Imogen's mother taking exception to an alcoholic firestarter being in charge of the school and Imogen still seeing Connor. Naturally Imogen's mother was not thrilled to learn that her daughter was now Mrs Mulgrew Jr, either. Angus Deayton properly arrived, as in he's now in the opening title sequence. He's gloriously offensive to everyone and has a high-maintenance Chinese wife. He put his name on the door of Grantly's classroom, which he's currently using. This made Verruca Salt and Harley have a meltdown because they revere Grantly and don't want him to die.

Maggie the Dinnerlady doesn't want him to die either, but the doctor said it was time to unplug him. Tom Clarkson tried not to heave a sigh of relief at the prospect that he could keep both his kidneys, and instead concentrated on looking tearful at the bedside (in what was actually a very sad scene). But then – a miracle! Grantly started breathing unaided. Maggie's prayers might have been answered after all, but Tom's grip on his second kidney is suddenly looking more shaky.

End of term, and the end of an era 5/7/2013

It was the last day of term at Waterloo Road, a day when traditionally the whole school comes together for an Event of some sort, and something goes very badly wrong.

Given that we knew Jason Done was done with Waterloo Road, the chances were high that the thing that went badly wrong would involve Tom Clarkson. For weeks my money has been on him dying on the operating table as he waved one of his kidneys off in the general direction of Grantly Budgen, but that's probably because I watch too much Holby.

Obviously things were more complicated than that, and it was going to be something to do with Kyle Stack, the disturbed youth with the hunted-animal eyes and the seductive dance moves (not on display here) who turned up at Waterloo Road fresh from prison and apparently ready to get himself some book learning.

Tom Clarkson wasn't thrilled to have Kyle on the premises, the old crossbow attack on Finn Sharkey in which The Lovely Josh got caught in the crossfire, and the gang warfare that almost resulted in Tariq's sister getting burned being fresh in his memory and so on. But his co-deputy head, Tactless Simon, reckoned he had a record of sorting out this kind of troubled youth.

So there was Kyle Stack wandering around like a caged wolf in a parka, requiring only a spot of goading from the always reliable Barry Barry to turn him from Mark Twain to violence. There were also a couple of red herrings in the form of the box of fireworks Tom kept carrying around ("Fireworks and Waterloo Road?" I said to PLA Jr. "That can't end well") and the cake Kyle Stack baked (poisoned, surely? But no. Angus Deayton ate it quite happily).

The real tragedy is that lessons have not been learned from the incident in which Harley almost jumped off the roof while under the influence of something potent and unspecified. Clearly access to the roof is still way too easy, as that's where Kyle Stack ended up, teetering on a parapet above the playground. And who was there to talk him down? Obviously it was Tom Clarkson, the man who's been in Waterloo Road since day one and has practically embodied the concept "pastoral care." He's seen the deaths of his wife, his girlfriend and his sort-of stepdaughter. He's had his sperm stolen and acquired an adorable son. He's offered a shoulder to cry on and a spare kidney to anyone who might need one.

And in one tragic slip, he's found himself crashing to the playground in front of the entire speaking cast and assorted extras. "Stay with me, Tom," pleaded Jane Beale, but it was too late.

If I'd been the director, I'd have had Nikki Boston setting off the fireworks just moments before, so Tom's demise would have had a backdrop of fizzing fireworks, rockets and explosions, and his beautiful eyes would have reflected pretty lights one last time. But I'm not the director (and just as well if I come up with clichéd nonsense like that). Instead we had the lonely figure of Kacey Barry kicking a football around in front of some graffiti saying "RIP Denzil" (the last spectacular WR death) and pondering a future without a man who always looked out for her and who was going to build a women's football team around her legendary skills.

And Grantly Budgen, speculating on the loss of a friend and – maybe – a kidney.

About the Author

Sue Haasler writes feel-good romantic comedies. Her first book, Two's Company, was published in the UK, France and Japan and was optioned for film by Warner Bros.

Novels by Sue Haasler:
Two's Company
Time After Time
True Colours
Better Than The Real Thing
Best Laid Plans (coming soon)

TV reviews
Holby City: Pauseliveaction's Reviews

Press and reader reviews for Sue's books:

[**Two's Company**] "A fresh, funny take on the chick-lit novel" (Hello!)
"I really enjoyed reading Two's Company. I think many women will relate to Anna." (IK, Japan)

[**Time After Time**] "I loved Time After Time so much that I did something I only do with really funny, wonderful books, I read it twice!" (JD, USA)
"I had a wonderful time remembering the songs, fashion and such from the 80s. Gideon was such a great hero." (KS, USA)

[**True Colours**] "The characters are lovely, the setting is beautiful, the story line is clever and whimsical." (GS, Scotland)

[**Better Than the Real Thing**] "I shall miss spending my evenings with Lia and discovering all the plot twists, none of which I had flagged. The heroine is wonderfully conflicted and the hero is so sweet and sexy." (BW, USA)

If you enjoyed this book, a quick review on Amazon would be very much appreciated. Thank you!

Website: www.suehaasler.com
Twitter: twitter.com/pauseliveaction
TV blog: www.pauseliveaction.com

Printed in Great Britain
by Amazon

51394625R00077